HIKES &
OUTINGS
of
South-Central
ONTARIO

N. Glenn Perrett

LONE
PINE

Lone Pine Publishing
2311 96 Street
Edmonton, Alberta T6N 1G3
Website: www.lonepinepublishing.com

Library and Archives Canada Cataloguing in Publication

Perrett, N. Glenn, 1960-
      Hikes & outings of South-Central Ontario / N. Glenn Perrett.

Includes bibliographical references.
ISBN 978-1-55105-884-9

      1. Day hiking—Ontario, South Central—Guidebooks.
I. Title II. Title: Hikes and outings of South-Central Ontario .

GV199.44.C22O58 2012   917.13'04   C2012-900957-1

Editorial Director: Nancy Foulds
Editorial: Wendy Pirk
Production Manager: Gene Longson
Layout and Production: Janina Kürschner, Volker Bodegom
Cover Design: Gerry Dotto
Cover Photograph: Glenn Perrett
Cartography: Volker Bodegom

Photography: All photos by Glenn, Gleannan, Lynn or Liam Perrett

Illustrations: Ted Nordhagen: 80; Gary Ross: 77, 128, 131, 143, 153, 180, 181, 186, 191, 194, 208, 210, 219; Ian Sheldon: 9, 38, 193.

We acknowledge the financial support of the Government of Canada through the Canada Book Fund (CBF) for our publishing activities.

All outdoor activities involve an element of risk. Weather, erosion and other forces may change the conditions or routes of a trail, and watercourses and waterfalls are inherently dangerous areas. Thus, keep in mind that this book serves as a guide only. It is the ultimate and sole responsibility of the reader to determine which areas are appropriate to his or her skills or fitness levels. Readers also hold the ultimate and sole responsibility to be aware of changes or hazards that might have occurred since the research and writing of this book.

PC: 16

Dedication

To Lynn, Gleannan and Liam—the best family you could ask for. May Nature remain an important part of your lives and receive the respect and protection that it deserves.

Acknowledgements

Numerous people contributed to the creation of this book—too many to list individually. I would like to thank the employees and volunteers of the various parks, conservation areas, trails and other wilderness areas who were generous with their time and willing to help out in a variety of ways.

Thanks to Andrew Promaine with Georgian Bay Islands National Park for showing our family numerous parts of the park and sharing his enthusiasm for this special place. Ron Knight was most gracious spending an afternoon providing us with a fascinating tour of the Trout Hollow Trail where John Muir and the Trout family lived and worked. I would also like to thank Chris Hamilton with the Hamilton Conservation Authority for his help, including his input in the chapter "Trail Etiquette and Safety." Chris Earley, a biologist with The Arboretum, University of Guelph, could always be counted on to help identify the plants and animals we photographed. Because Chris only identified some of the plants and animals in this book, I take responsibility if any species are incorrectly identified. Thanks Chris!

Our family tends to get lost easily, so we were delighted when GPS Central (www.gps-central.ca) provided us with a handheld GPS unit loaded with topographic and road maps. This device was valuable in getting us to and from the wilderness areas as well as while we explored them.

I would like to thank Lone Pine Publishing for publishing this book and those who worked on this project including Wendy Pirk, Nancy Foulds, Volker Bodegom and Janina Kürschner.

Relatives who accompanied us on some of the nature treks made these outings enjoyable and include my brothers Neil and Keith, my cousin Ian and my parents-in-law, Bob and Audrey. Thanks also go to my parents, Helen and Norman, who deserve much of the credit for my developing a love of, and respect for, nature.

I also need to acknowledge the trees that were used in the production of this book. We need to return to using plants, such as hemp, for much of our paper needs so that forests can be preserved.

Finally, a big thank you to my wonderful family whose enjoyment of nature made this project both educational and fun. Together we took the photos featured in this book. Lynn was helpful in reviewing the chapters and selecting photographs while Gleannan's and Liam's feedback regarding the nature outings was valuable. Sharing the wilderness experiences in this book with Liam, Gleannan and Lynn was special and something I will cherish for the rest of my life.

TABLE OF

CONTENTS

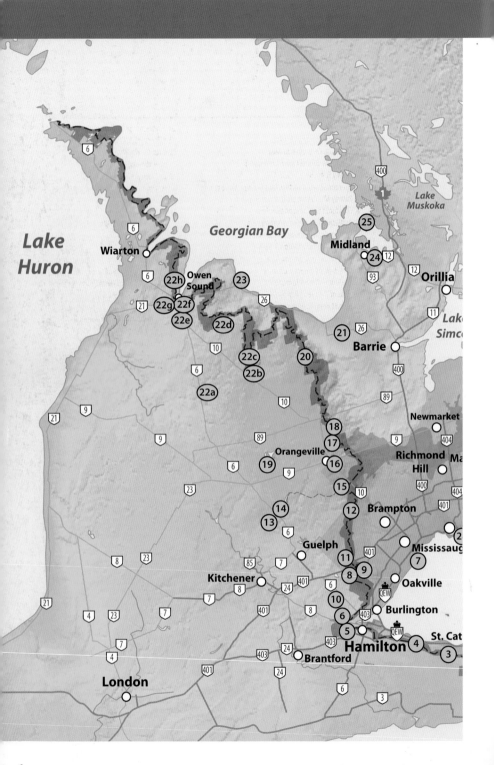

1 The Bruce Trail
2 Woodend Conservation Area
3 Ball's Falls Conservation Area
4 Beamer Memorial Conservation Area
5 Tiffany Falls Conservation Area
6 Spencer Gorge/Webster's Falls Conservation Area
7 Rattray Marsh Conservation Area
8 Crawford Lake Conservation Area
9 Rattlesnake Point Conservation Area
10 Fletcher Creek Ecological Preserve
11 Hilton Falls Conservation Area
12 Terra Cotta Conservation Area
13 Elora Gorge Conservation Area
14 The Elora Cataract Trailway
15 Forks of the Credit Provincial Park
16 Island Lake Conservation Area
17 Hockley Valley Provincial Nature Reserve
18 Mono Cliffs Provincial Park
19 Luther Marsh Wildlife Management Area

20 Nottawasaga Bluffs Conservation Area
21 Minesing Wetlands
22 Grey County Waterfalls
  a McGowan Falls
  b Hoggs Falls
  c Eugenia Falls
  d Walters Falls
  e Inglis Falls
  f Weavers Creek Falls
  g Jones Falls
  h Indian Falls
23 Meaford
24 Wye Marsh Wildlife Centre
25 Georgian Bay Islands National Park
26 Oak Ridges Moraine
27 Rouge Park
28 Tommy Thompson Park
29 Thickson's Woods
30 Presqu'ile Provincial Park

Orillia
Lake Simcoe
Lake Muskoka
Newmarket
Markham
Whitby
Oshawa
Ajax
Pickering
Clarington
Cobourg
Clarington
Peterborough
Lake Scugog
Rice Lake
Belleville
Toronto
Mississauga
Oakville
Burlington
St. Catharines
Niagara Falls
Buffalo
Rochester
Lake Ontario

Richmond Hill

401 — main highway
9 — secondary highway
20 — hike number
— — — Bruce Trail
— · — · — Elora Cataract Trailway
O O city, town
Greater Toronto Area
Niagara Escarpment
Oak Ridges Moraine

N

Introduction

I spent much of my early childhood in Sarnia, a short walk from Lake Huron. Our backyard contained beautiful black locust trees, and there were plenty of nearby woods and fields to explore, not to mention the shores of Lake Huron. It was an ideal natural setting for a young boy to grow up in. When I was 10 our family moved to Thornhill, and though there were not as many "wild" spaces to explore, there were woods, fields and an interesting creek not too far from our house.

In the mid-1960s my parents purchased a scenic lot on Georgian Bay, where they had a cottage built. For most of my childhood, I spent the entire summer at this wonderful place. I would go to the cottage the day school ended for the summer and stay there until Labour Day. Two glorious months to swim, walk in the woods and canoe the spectacular shorelines of the bays and islands.

A long bay next to the bay our cottage was on was one of my favourite places to canoe. The approximately 3-kilometre

bay features four islands. At the end of the bay is a small, sheltered bay accessible through some narrows. I've always referred to this quiet spot as "the inland lake," and it was one of my favourite places to explore.

Canoeing to the inland lake was always interesting. I would paddle along the sheltered shores of the islands, looking for animals on the land and fish in the waters. Before entering the inland lake, I would sit quietly in the canoe at the shallow narrows. Here you could observe fish entering and leaving

the shallow, weedy bay through the sandy narrows. After lingering at this spot for a while, I would slowly and quietly canoe the perimeter of the bay, reacquainting myself with an old friend.

I spent hours in this special ecosystem which, for its small size, contained an incredible diversity of fish species including northern pike, smallmouth bass, rock bass, largemouth bass, pumpkinseed, black crappie, brown bullhead, common carp, yellow perch, rainbow trout, burbot and longnose gar. Within the bay itself there were

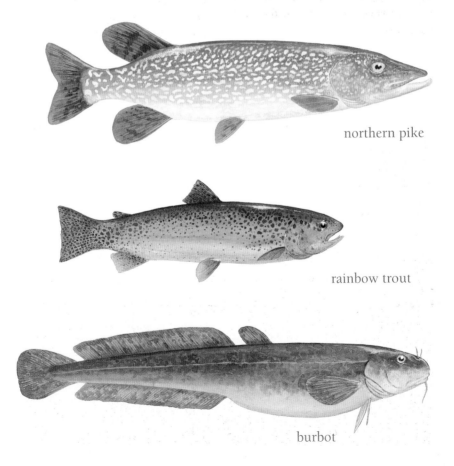

northern pike

rainbow trout

burbot

some deeper, sandy spots as well as shallow areas where lily pads and other plants transformed the bay into an aquatic garden.

A beaver dam next to a rock was a favourite spot of mine, as was the end of the bay where I would pull the canoe on shore, climb a rocky slope and look out over the water to watch the fish swimming among the aquatic plants. After spending hours at this special place, I would return to the cottage by canoeing the far, virtually cottage-free, shore of the bay.

When I wasn't canoeing to the inland lake, I was exploring the numerous bays and islands by canoe. In the evening when the wind died down, slowly paddling the rocky shorelines with their towering pine trees was a great way to end the day.

I eagerly looked forward to spending summers at the cottage where I could live and play in a natural environment.

Although I haven't spent much time there during the last couple of decades, my parents' cottage still holds many very special memories for me. It was significant in creating and moulding my respect for, and love of, the natural world, and I wanted my family to grow up in a similar setting. My wife, Lynn, who was also raised in a family that enjoyed nature, held similar beliefs. It's

not surprising that the home where we decided to live and raise our family is in a natural setting featuring meadows, woods and wetlands that are surrounded by forests, streams and rivers. Trails allow us to enjoy this special place without disturbing the plants and animals who also make the area their home. Because we also wanted to spend part of the year on a lake, we purchased a scenic lot on a large lake northeast of Parry Sound. We enjoy exploring the magnificent shoreline and its rugged environs.

I have been fortunate to spend a lot of my life in rural Ontario, but you don't have to live in the countryside or have a cottage to enjoy nature. If you do live in a natural setting, you will benefit from getting out into different wilderness areas and seeing the incredible

diversity and scenery that we often take for granted in Ontario. Whether you live in a small town, a big city or in the country, there are many advantages to getting off the couch and exploring the myriad trails, forests, wetlands and other protected wilderness areas.

During the last few years, our family has visited numerous wilderness areas close to our home near Mansfield. Many of these places we didn't even know existed until recently when we discovered them on our own on the Internet. Once we were hiking the trails and exploring conservation areas, provincial and national parks and other protected areas, we discovered more places we wanted to investigate. Such was the case when we were enjoying Beautiful Joe Park in Meaford and saw a sign for Trout Hollow Trail. With a little research I learned that this trail went through Trout Hollow on the Bighead River. It was here that John Muir, a pioneer of the conservation movement, spent a year and a half from 1864

to 1866 working for the Trout family. The Trout Hollow Trail is on mostly private land and Ron Knight, who owns the property where John Muir lived and worked, graciously spent an afternoon

● *John Muir*

PERMITTED USES:

TRAIL ETIQUETTE:
• This trail is primarily on private land. respect the property, wildlife and wildflowers.
• Keep your garbage with you and don't litter.
• Obey trail closure signs and caution signs.
• Stay on the trail.
• Expect and respect other users.

TRAIL MARKERS:
GREEN - EASY WALKING
YELLOW - MODERATE
RED - DIFFICULT

USE THIS TRAIL AT YOUR OWN RISK
MANAGED BY THE BIGHEAD RIVER HERITAGE ASSOCIATION
www.bigheadriver.org

giving our family a fascinating tour and history lesson.

The more you experience nature, the more you appreciate and respect it. You also meet like-minded nature lovers who are often delighted to spend a moment or two exchanging advice about places to visit—and in south-central Ontario there is no shortage of places to go in spite of our misguided attempts to alter the natural landscape.

After leaving a scenic nature area where we had an enjoyable hike, I noticed how close to civilization this island of wilderness was. Leaving the parking lot, tired but invigorated, we could see a major

highway close by. After a few minutes of driving, we were in the industrial sector of one of the fastest growing areas in Canada. There is little chance of this vital piece of nature expanding much, if at all. Let's just hope that people realize its importance and do not allow it to decrease in size in the future. Humans need more interaction with nature, not less.

Our family has benefitted from the wide array of environmental experiences we've enjoyed literally at our doorstep. From waterfalls and parks in large urban centres to wetlands and nature preserves in rural areas, this book covers numerous spots that we have visited in the south-central part of the province.

And these places are only the tip of the iceberg. After reading about, and visiting, some of the areas where we have spent time conversing with nature, discover some of your own special places where you can hike, bike, canoe or simply marvel at the beauty of the natural world.

Making good use of these protected natural areas and using them responsibly will help ensure their survival. A bigger population means an increase in development and more pressure to transform meadows, forests and wetlands into roads, malls and subdivisions. Southern Ontario has already lost 80 percent or more of its pre-settlement wetlands, which has resulted in poor water quality, a loss of biodiversity and increased flooding.

But an increase in population also means that we need to increase, not decrease, natural areas. Wilderness is crucial in maintaining biodiversity, a healthy environment and our health. Various studies show that nature improves our physical and psychological well-being and even helps us intellectually. Nature also relaxes us and can improve communication between family members and friends.

Your nature experiences will benefit you in a variety of ways. Spending time in these relatively untouched environments will also increase the respect that you have for these wilderness areas. With this greater respect comes a stronger desire to use and protect these islands of nature and that is what is desperately needed.

N. Glenn Perrett

The Need for Nature

Let children walk with Nature, let them see the beautiful blendings and communions of death and life, their joyous inseparable unity...

—John Muir

Numerous studies and reports in recent years indicate that Canadian children and adults do not get enough exercise and that childhood obesity is on the rise. Statistics Canada, in partnership with the Public Health Agency of Canada and Health Canada, started the "Canadian Health Measures Survey" in 2007. The survey found evidence that in the past few decades, the health of Canadian children has deteriorated, childhood obesity has risen and physical fitness has declined. The survey also found that only 15 percent of Canadian adults were getting as much physical activity as they should be.

The situation does not appear to be any better in the United States; in fact, it may be worse. In the foreword of Rebecca P. Cohen's book *15 Minutes Outside: 365 Ways to Get Out of the House and Connect With Your Kids*, Dr. Tererai Trent cites the U.S. Department of Health and Human Services when stating that "...the rate of childhood obesity in the United States has more than tripled in the past thirty years."

Cohen supports these findings: "One in three children is obese. The average child spends more than thirty hours in front of television and electronics

a week and gets only four to seven minutes a day of unstructured playtime outside."

And though I haven't done any studies or surveys on children, adults and exercise, I agree with these findings based on my observations over the years. When I was growing up in Sarnia and Thornhill in the 1960s and '70s, ball hockey games were common in our neighbourhood. During winter, the rink that my mother made each year was well used by my brothers and me along with our friends as we played hockey for hours. A couple of strategically placed lights allowed us to continue until well past dark. During spring and fall, my friends and I would ride our bikes, play sports or do other activities outdoors. Summers I spent at our cottage where I swam, canoed, explored the forests and walked the country roads.

Today children seem to spend little time exercising and lots of time playing with electronics. Many kids, and adults, have embraced and become caught in our increasingly high-tech society. The constant texting of messages and talking to friends on cell phones, social networking, playing video games, listening to mp3 players, surfing the Internet and watching television have replaced exercise and play—especially outdoors. There are many repercussions of this change in how we use our leisure time. Besides a loss in the art of conversation, our health

suffers and we become increasingly disconnected from nature.

This disconnect from nature and its consequences were addressed by Richard Louv in his bestselling book *Last Child in the Woods: Saving Our Children from Nature-Deficit Disorder* and, more recently, in his book *The Nature Principle: Human Restoration and the End of Nature-Deficit Disorder.*

In *Last Child in the Woods,* Louv introduced the term "nature-deficit disorder." According to Louv, "Nature-deficit disorder describes the human costs of alienation from nature, among them: diminished use of the senses, attention difficulties, and higher rates of physical and emotional illnesses."

In his books, Louv states that nature may help those with attention deficit hyperactivity disorder (ADHD) and provides considerable information that nature has a positive effect on our mental, physical and even spiritual health.

According to the report *Nature Nurtures: Investigating the Potential of School Grounds* by Evergreen—a charitable organization that makes cities more liveable—greener, more nature-oriented school grounds improve the academic performances of students and increase the teachers' enthusiasm for teaching. The report cites numerous other benefits for students, teachers, schools and communities when school grounds are made more natural by introducing meadows, trees, shrubs and gardens.

It would appear that the benefits associated with spending time in nature are both numerous and varied. Besides the benefits already mentioned, nature and trees reduces stress and improves our ability to concentrate. Patients with a view of nature spend less time in the hospital compared to patients who didn't have a view of nature during their hospital stay.

Of course spending time in nature usually involves exercise, such as hiking, which also has numerous health benefits—both physical and psychological. Benefits include preventing heart disease, lowering cholesterol levels, improving mental health such as depression and stress, controlling and preventing diabetes, improving arthritis and even helping with osteoporosis.

And as John Muir points out in the quotation at the beginning of this chapter, nature teaches us about life.

Another positive aspect of getting out into nature is that it can improve communication and relationships between family members. Families have become victims of our high-tech society with little quality time given to family activities. Outdoor natural settings can encourage children, parents and grandparents to open up and share conversations, concerns, ideas and problems, resulting in better communication and important family bonding opportunities that will create greater family cohesion.

An enjoyable family nature outing has so many benefits. During the last decade Lynn, Liam, Gleannan and I have hiked scenic forests, explored wetlands by canoe, skied and snowshoed snow-covered trails and hiked and swam on a beautiful island in Georgian Bay.

The quality time spent exploring these wilderness areas was wonderful. Each environmental trek was educational, entertaining and great exercise. When we were finished visiting these nature areas, we were tired, but it was a good tired. Each excursion not only provided us with fascinating nature experiences, but also with fond memories and nice photographs.

As rewarding as these wilderness trips were, they weren't expensive; many cost only the gas we used to drive to the scenic spots. What we received in return—well, you can't put a price on that.

Preserving the Memories

Not all who wander are lost.

—J. R. R. Tolkien

A nice family outing in a scenic park or other wilderness area is something you will want to remember. And while such fond experiences often become cherished memories that you can recall from time to time for the rest of your life, you may want a little help remembering these fun times in the outdoors.

Digital cameras are relatively inexpensive compared to the old film cameras—at least on a cost-per-photograph basis. Because there is no film to buy and develop, we tend to take hundreds of photographs every time we go on a nature excursion.

We generally use at least two cameras, and we often snap the same picturesque landscape, beautiful flower or fascinating animal numerous times on different settings. When we get home we go through the photos on the computer, delete those that didn't turn out and file the others. Some of those stored in the computer occasionally remind us of a particular hike, canoe trip or similar activity from a nature experience because they are part of our screen saver.

Photographs we are particularly fond of we have developed and framed or put in a photo album. Keeping photo albums for your children, as well as yourself, is a nice way to preserve memories of your wilderness treks with your family.

Years later, when family members gather, you can reminisce about past adventures in nature by looking at a selection of the photographs. Not only will you have received the many benefits of getting out and exercising in the natural world in the first place, but you now have tangible memories of those happy times.

While photographs are a good way to keep memories, so too is taking home movies of your nature outings. Family movies are fun to watch—especially years later.

Keeping a journal is another way to preserve memories of special events in your life, including spending time in parks and hiking trails with your family. Maintaining a written record of your family's visits to forests, marshes, rivers and other habitats is fun. Keeping such a record can be therapeutic and relaxing. Reading old journal entries brings back wonderful memories—and your written thoughts can be handed down to your children and grandchildren to read.

Enjoying nature with family is a wonderful way to spend time together and create memories that will last a lifetime.

A Bit About This Book

It seems to me that we all look at Nature too much,
and live with her too little.

—Oscar Wilde

The nature areas selected for this book are quite different in many ways, but they have some things in common. They are located within an approximately 90 minute drive of the Greater Toronto Area (GTA) and they are in south-central Ontario. They are also good examples of wilderness areas in southern Ontario.

In fact, many of the wilderness areas have been recognized with any of a number of designations including an Area of Natural and Scientific Interest (ANSI). Earth Science and Life Science ANSI's are areas identified by the Ontario Ministry of Natural Resources as having provincially or regionally

significant geological (Earth Science) or ecological (Life Science) features. Other designations have been given by different levels of government and international bodies and pertain to various important areas including wetlands and habitat for animals.

One of the more difficult things about writing this book (besides trying to convey in words how special the wilderness areas featured in this book are) was deciding what to include and what to leave out. If you are looking for places to go that are commercial in nature, this book is not for you. Families need to connect, or reconnect, with nature and get exercise without spending a lot of money, so expensive nature areas and experiences were not included in these pages. Some of the wilderness areas featured here are free; others have modest user fees, parking fees or additional fees associated with specific activities.

Because so much time and effort goes into making a book, and trees are killed to make the paper, I didn't want the information to be out of date within a few years. For this reason I have intentionally kept some information vague or excluded it altogether. For example, I have not mentioned user fees for the parks, if there are any, because they can change relatively frequently. At least one website is included for each chapter, and these websites offer current information on various things including user fees and trail information. It is a good idea to visit these websites when you are planning a visit to these areas.

There is a map that shows where the nature areas featured in the book are located. You can use this map to plan out multiple places in an area to visit on a trip. Some of the places you will not be able to adequately cover in a single visit, whereas you could comfortably visit two or three smaller areas in a day. If you plan to go away for a holiday or a weekend, you can use this map to help you choose several places for your nature excursion.

Besides the map, the chapters of the nature areas will help you decide when and where to go on a particular nature outing. The order of the chapters in the book is similar to where the areas exist geographically. I start in the south in the Niagara region, head north and northwest of the GTA before coming back south and taking in some nature areas east of the GTA. Chapters close to one another in the book will usually be in the same geographic area, as well.

Individual maps have not been used as they are often outdated shortly after being created—trails change, are closed or rerouted, and with each of these changes the book becomes less accurate. Many of the websites provided in this book feature good trail maps and/or provide up-to-date trail information, so you can access these sites for such information. The websites also have contact information, and it is a good idea to contact the areas in advance of your visit to see if they can send you any maps, brochures or other information that will make your nature outing more informative and enjoyable. Some of the nature areas offer guided hikes and other activities that are worth finding out about.

You should also know when parks, and the other nature areas in the book, are open and what their hours are. Sometimes hours change depending on the season. You don't want to travel to a park or conservation area anticipating a fun outing only to be disappointed. For example, Tommy Thompson Park in Toronto is a wonderful place to visit, but it is only open to the public on weekends and some holidays, so do your homework before leaving home.

Internet searches can help you get more information about the places you are interested in seeing. Visiting nature

TRAIL CLOSED

BRUCE TRAIL

NO HIKING

NEW TRAIL TO THE RIGHT

areas is educational and a lot of fun, but so is learning more about them before you go there. And don't forget to contact other agencies for information. When I contacted Grey County Tourism about their waterfall tour, they mailed me a brochure that contained information about, and directions to, each of the waterfalls on the tour. They also sent a detailed map of Grey County. These publications were extremely useful and made the wonderful tour even more enjoyable.

Written directions are provided for each of the nature areas in the book. It is a good idea to map out your own directions prior to setting out as you may be coming from a different direction. Road names change, too, and some roads are known by more than one name or are given a different name in a different section of the road. Directions are often on the website for the nature area, and sometimes GPS coordinates or an address are also provided. You can also contact the nature area to get specific directions for where you are coming from. Many of the nature areas have signs you can follow when you start getting close to your destination.

In this book, I have divided the day-trip chapters into two parts. The first part of the chapter deals with the characteristics of the nature area and includes such information as its size, the habitats and species found there, activities allowed as well as some of its history and geography. The second part of the chapter is a personal account of our family's experience there—when we went, what areas we visited, what we saw and what we liked about it. This information, combined with the photographs, should provide you with a good idea of what the nature area is like. At the beginning of each chapter there is a section called At a Glance, which provides you with a quick glimpse of some of the main features for that area.

Although you can read the book from beginning to end, I have written each chapter to be a complete look at the nature area featured. For this reason, similar information will occasionally be found in more than one chapter. To help ensure the accuracy of the information provided for the parks and conservation areas covered, each chapter has been reviewed by at least one representative of the nature area featured. While I have been thorough in researching this book and have taken many precautions to ensure its accuracy, I apologize in advance for any mistakes.

Before heading out, please read the Trail Etiquette and Safety section. Many of the nature areas in this book are environmentally sensitive or contain rare or endangered species. Visiting these areas while minimizing your impact on the environment is important. Also, dangerous sites are common in many of the nature areas, and you should be aware of these and how to keep yourself and your family safe.

I have written this book for families wanting to get out and enjoy the many benefits of nature, but it applies to anyone who wants to commune with nature. Enjoy.

Trail Etiquette and Safety

The greatness of a nation and its moral progress can be judged by the way its animals are treated.

—Mohandas Gandhi

Before you go visiting wilderness areas, whether you are hiking, cross-country skiing, snowshoeing or doing some other activity, make sure you are fit enough to safely accomplish these nature excursions. Don't select trails that are too difficult, don't walk for longer than you are comfortably able to walk, and wear appropriate footwear and clothing. If you are not sure about your conditioning, check with your doctor before setting out. When you do exercise on the trails, start slowly and work your way up to longer and more demanding trails.

One of the most important things to remember when visiting wilderness areas is that your nature outing is taking place in the homes of others. To protect the flora and fauna, as well as the environment and your family, there are some basic rules and guidelines to remember and follow.

Trail Etiquette

Stay on the marked trails. Trails often go through environmentally sensitive areas or places with rare and endangered species, and it is important not to go off the trails where you might harm plants or animals or damage the environment. The trails also go through land belonging to parks, conservation authorities, organizations and private individuals, and it is important to respect these properties.

Leave the trails as you found them—unless you improve them by removing garbage that you come across—and

educate your children about the importance of keeping wilderness areas as pristine as possible. Look at, but don't touch or disturb, the plants and animals who live there. The saying about taking only photographs and leaving only footprints is a good rule to live by when hiking.

Be courteous of others. Allow room when passing other hikers, and don't be too noisy—many people escape to wilderness areas to enjoy the quiet and solitude. Being reasonably quiet will also help to ensure that you don't disturb animals.

Do not feed the wildlife.

Hiking With Dogs

Hiking with a canine companion is fun and good exercise, but there are many things that you should consider before taking to the trails with your "best friend." Are dogs allowed in the nature area that you plan on visiting? Some parks and conservation areas allow dogs, but others do not. Some areas restrict where the dogs can go or insist that they have to be on a leash, and some even specify the length of leash that is allowed, such as a maximum of 2 metres. It is wise to check ahead to learn what is allowed when it comes to dogs.

If you do take your dog on your nature outings, ensure that she is fit enough to accompany you. Check with your dog's veterinarian before setting out. You may have to get your dog in better condition by taking her for frequent, shorter walks and gradually building up her conditioning and stamina

before going on a longer hike. Make sure that you also take your dog's age into account.

Dogs should wear a collar or a harness and be on a leash. Leashes help you keep your dog safe. Dogs allowed to run loose can scare, harm or get into altercations with other animals, and they can fall into rivers or gorges, go over waterfalls or meet some other unfortunate fate in the wilderness. They can also run off and become lost. Many people are also frightened of dogs, even the friendliest of canines, so keep your pet on a leash when visiting nature areas.

If your dog is not well trained, is old or is not in good shape, it may be best to leave him at home when you go hiking.

If you do take your canine companion on a nature outing, make sure that she is up-to-date with her vaccinations, that she doesn't suffer from heatstroke, frostbite or hyperthermia and that you clean up after her. Take along water and, depending on how long you are going for, food or snacks for her. Collapsible water and food bowls are available and easy to carry. Some first aid items for your dog can also be a good idea, even if you are only going for part of the day.

Effective identification is always important and should contain your phone number and address. Our dogs' tags are made by LuckyPet and are affixed to their collars with a durable "O" ring (more secure than an "S" ring). Each tag contains our dog's name, our name, address and phone number, and LuckyPet's

toll-free phone number. LuckyPet has an Owner Alert! pet recovery service that allows you to provide alternate phone numbers, such as for your work or cell phone or even temporary numbers if you are travelling, to be sure that if anyone finds your missing pet, LuckyPet can get in touch with you.

Some Items to Consider Taking

While day trips don't require the planning and equipment that longer trips into the wilderness warrant, some items should be still be taken along.

It is a good idea to dress in layers so you can add or remove layers as necessary. Clothes should be comfortable, and consider taking rainwear or at least

a lightweight, folding umbrella if rain is in the forecast. We take plastic bags for extra protection for our cameras if there is the possibility of rain. Hiking boots or durable running shoes are also important. A second pair of socks is recommended.

Other items to consider taking on day trips include a first-aid kit, a hat that offers good protection from the sun, an emergency whistle, a flashlight, water (one of the most important items), nutritious snacks, sunglasses, a compass and/or GPS, a cell phone for emergencies, a pocketknife, protection from the sun and bugs, a camera and a backpack to carry everything.

Safety First

Although the nature areas featured in this book are in south-central Ontario and not in remote parts of the province, it is always a good idea not to go alone in the wilderness. If you do go by yourself, let someone know where you are going, when you plan to leave and when you expect to return.

Protect yourself from ticks because the blacklegged tick can spread Lyme disease through its bite. You can reduce the chances of being bitten by a tick by wearing long pants tucked into your socks and a long-sleeved shirt. Wearing light-coloured clothing will allow you to better see ticks on your clothes.

Many of the parks, conservation areas and trails are on the Niagara Escarpment, where there are steep cliffs and rocky areas, so exercise extreme caution at all times. Children need to be educated about the dangers in the nature areas you visit and kept out of harm's way. Stay away from the edges of cliffs and other steep drops. Keep your dog on a leash. Stay on the marked trails and pay attention to signs—particularly signs that indicate potentially dangerous situations. Never throw anything over cliffs, waterfalls and similar areas because there may be people below.

Many of the areas in the book have waterfalls, which despite their beauty are dangerous places if you are not careful. Do not go into waters upstream of waterfalls because the rocks are often slippery, being covered in algae, and unstable. If you lose your balance, you can be swept downstream and over the falls. Streams and creeks can have dangerous currents, and the current upstream of a waterfall can suddenly increase as a result of rain or if a dam is opened. It is also unsafe at the foot of waterfalls because of water flow, loose, slippery rocks and objects, such as logs, falling over the falls. View waterfalls from safe locations such as from the trails and lookouts.

For those who canoe or kayak, make sure you are experienced for the conditions that you will be in and that you wear a lifejacket or personal flotation device and have at least the minimum boat safety equipment required.

A few of the areas featured in this book allow hunting at certain times of the year. Be aware when hunting and other dangerous activities occur, and take the appropriate steps to ensure that you and your family are not placed in a potentially dangerous situation.

Preserving and Creating Wild Places

*We are born out of wildness, exactly like the other animals
(and plants), and civilization is only there to help us after the fact.
Polluting the wildness is a way of making it unwild,
of breaking it, squeezing it by sheer force until it mutates.
As we begin to own and control it, we lose it,
because it is no longer the same thing:
its independence is gone, the magic is covered with soot.*

—Robert Hunter

We have grown up in an era where weedless, neatly trimmed lawns with non-native trees, shrubs and flowers are the norm. These chemically dependent, monoculture lawns and ornamental, non-native plants are admired while pesticide- and herbicide-free lawns consisting of native wildflowers and trees, with some dandelions, are frowned upon.

Although society is slowly becoming more accepting of dandelions and other harmless plants—particularly as we become more enlightened about the devastating long-term consequences

associated with pesticides, herbicides and other toxic chemicals—we still have a long way to go. It is still common for people to turn rural properties consisting of numerous native trees, plants and animals into giant lawns. What was once a healthy ecosystem with high plant and animal diversity then becomes an unhealthy piece of land largely devoid of life.

A new philosophy is needed—one in which native plants and animals are protected and their needs met. An easy way to foster a more natural environment is to create wild places. Whether you have a small yard or a large property, there are many ways to create wild places without spending much time or money.

One of the easiest ways is to allow the land to return to a more natural environment on its own. You can also assist Mother Nature by planting some native trees, bushes and flowers. Native plants require less water than non-native species, and they are more adapted to the area. Using native plants, shrubs and trees also provides food, shelter and habitat for insects and other animals, as well as minimizes the spread of non-native species.

In his book *Bringing Nature Home: How Native Plants Sustain Wildlife in Our Gardens*, Douglas W. Tallamy points out the importance of using native plants because insects do not feed on non-native species, which results

in consequences that affect the entire ecosystem.

"If our native insect fauna cannot, or will not, use alien plants for food, then insect populations in areas with many alien plants will be smaller than insect populations in areas with all natives. This may sound like a gardener's dream: a land without insects! But because so many animals depend partially or entirely on insect protein for food, a land without insects is a land without most forms of higher life."

Our family home consists of 10 hectares of woods, wetlands and meadows. Over the years we have planted thousands of native trees and allowed land cleared in past decades to return to a more natural state on its own. Transplanting young trees is another easy way to help reforest an area. Moving young trees growing in a vulnerable location to a more advantageous spot helps the young trees and the environment. On our property, trees that benefit from being relocated include seedlings that are growing on trails and young trees that are growing in very close proximity to one another.

We have also minimized our intrusion on the different habitats by creating some modest trails and keeping these footpaths well away from wetlands and other environmentally sensitive areas. The trails go around large trees, and if small trees needed to be moved, they were carefully transplanted a short distance off the path. The trails allow us to visit the different areas without disturbing plants and animals, because this natural area is their home too. During winter we cross-country ski on these trails, which are also used by other animals. Tracks from coyotes, deer, foxes and rabbits commonly grace these popular routes.

Protecting or creating a wild place, no matter how small, is important. Planting native wildflowers in a corner of your yard will attract butterflies and bees, providing the animals with food and increasing species diversity. Planting native trees provides shelter, homes and food for animals. Even organic vegetable gardens are useful "wild" places that will attract animals such as toads and insects. Just make sure if you have animal companions that you don't plant species that are toxic to them unless the plants are inaccessible to your four-legged family members.

If many homeowners created wild places in their yards, there would be nature corridors in urban and suburban areas where species could live and travel. Such backyard habitat corridors would provide increased immigration between areas allowing for increased

coyote tracks

populations, less inbreeding, more foraging areas and increased species diversity.

Educating neighbours about the need to establish wild places is also important. Just remind them that such areas have many environmental benefits and usually require less work to maintain.

By returning even a small portion of the land to a more natural state, we help species diversity, combat global warming and reduce our ecological footprint. We can't own the land—it is for all species; but we can become responsible stewards of it. And this responsibility doesn't have to be a costly one. Planting a single oak tree can provide food, shelter and homes for numerous animals, reduce carbon dioxide and provide oxygen for the next several hundred years.

Respecting and Protecting Wetlands

In one respect every natural area has a common uniqueness—
it takes everyone forever to preserve it,
but one person and one time to destroy it.

—E. J. Koestner

Wetlands are lands that are permanently or seasonally wet and, in Ontario, consist of marshes, swamps, fens, bogs and shallow open water. Marshes are productive wetlands that are rich in nutrients and feature standing or slowly moving water. They are also a source of oxygen and, as with other natural areas, they provide corridors for animals and plants to travel. Cattails and reeds are common plants of marshes. Swamps are also rich in nutrients; they contain trees and shrubs and are flooded seasonally or for long periods of time. Bogs are peat-covered wetlands common in northern Ontario; sphagnum mosses are common, but trees may also be present. Fens feature high water tables and contain sedges and sometimes trees and shrubs. Shallow open water includes potholes and ponds as well as waters along lakeshores and rivers.

Wetlands are some of the most important and productive ecosystems on Earth—and they are also some of the most fragile and least respected. Many people still consider these vital places as little more than mosquito-infested wastelands that need to be filled in and developed. As a result of such ignorance, and greed, 80% or more of southern Ontario's pre-settlement wetlands have been destroyed. This loss has resulted in a variety of environmental ills, including reduced biodiversity, poor water quality and increased flooding.

Wetlands provide numerous functions that we know of and likely many others of which we are unaware. They purify water by removing contaminants, suspended particles and excessive nutrients, such as phosphates. They also provide habitat for many species of plants, birds, mammals, reptiles, amphibians and fish.

Often overlooked is the vital role that wetlands play in controlling flooding. They act as reservoirs, soaking up excess water, such as after a rain, and slowly releasing it during drier seasons. This both controls flooding and eases the affects of drought. Wetlands also minimize soil erosion by slowing runoff from storms and thaws.

Another crucial function of wetlands is the role these ecosystems play as a source of oxygen. They also help out with global warming by retaining carbon from decaying plants and animals.

Wetlands also provide us with wonderful recreational opportunities such as hiking, canoeing and bird watching.

We have a seasonal stream on our property along with other wetlands and a vernal pool. Vernal pools contain water for part of the year, gathering it from rains and snowmelt, and dry up later in the summer. Because vernal pools dry out, they don't have populations of fish, making them good habitat for frogs, toads, salamanders and other amphibians to breed and have their young. "Our" vernal pool is home to various species of frogs, toads and other animals and plants. Even if your wetland consists of only a small area of cattails, make sure that you protect it.

Wetlands face numerous threats. Many have been filled in for land development or drained for agricultural purposes. People frequently purchase ecologically sensitive wetlands and then destroy them by bringing in fill to landscape the property, build a house and install a driveway. Ponds are often created in wetlands, or already established ponds are enlarged. In the process, native trees and plants are removed and are replaced with non-native species and lawns.

Other factors affecting wetlands include pollution from agricultural, industrial, commercial and other sources, artificial changes in water levels, the removal of shoreline vegetation and climate change.

Although wetlands are in jeopardy, there are ways to protect these eco-systems. If you are fortunate enough to have streams, ponds, marshes or other wetlands on your property, be a good steward and keep them healthy. This is usually best accomplished by leaving the wetlands, and the areas surrounding them, alone.

You can also save wetland ecosystems by speaking out when you witness them being destroyed or damaged by contacting the proper authorities. Contact politicians and write letters to the editor of local newspapers and magazines.

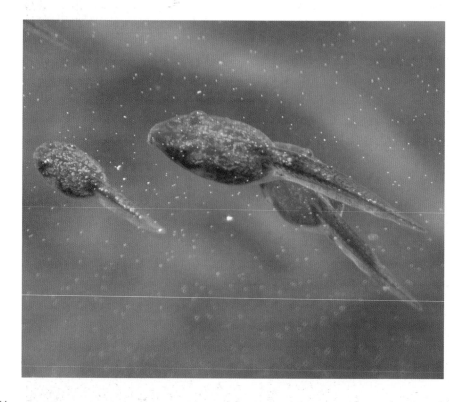

Educating children about wetlands may be the most important way to preserve these special places. When it comes to protecting the areas that remain in southern Ontario, future generations will have to be wiser and more respectful of streams, ponds, marshes and other wetlands.

Enjoying Ontario's Autumn Colours

The clearest way into the universe is through a forest wilderness.

—John Muir

■ Hiking a forest trail in autumn is a wonderful way to spend part of a day. Moderate temperatures and a lack of biting insects add to the beautiful scenery at this time of year—especially when the trees start to change colour. Sunny days combined with cool nights help to transform Ontario's spectacular green forests into stunning palettes of yellow, orange, gold, red and purple. Although these colourful landscapes are short lived, it is worth making arrangements to visit areas where autumn's brilliant displays of colour are exhibited.

Trees change colour around the world, but autumn's tapestry of colour that occurs in Ontario, Quebec and the northeastern United States is second to none. From early to mid-September enough trees have started to turn colour that people are anticipating the time, usually in October, when deciduous forests are dressed in their autumn finest. The myriad colours, displayed among the dark greens of coniferous trees, are a sight to behold.

The intensity of colours is influenced by a variety of things, including temperature and sunlight. Autumns that are sunny and warm during the day with cool nights produce leaves with plenty of colour, whereas cold, rainy autumns often result in dull brown and yellow leaves that fall from the trees earlier than usual. Whether the colours are brilliant or dull, they are short lived. A couple of windy days will have many of the leaves lying on the ground, where they will decompose and return nutrients to the soil.

Because autumn's colours don't last long, it is wise to plan where you will enjoy the display—and don't forget to take your camera. Photographs of trails as well as autumn landscapes are stunning and make nice keepsakes of an enjoyable day spent in nature. You can monitor the state of the autumn colours by visiting local hardwood forests or by accessing websites that provide information on how the colours are progressing in various areas.

Autumn's constantly changing colours are a joy to behold, but why do leaves change colour and fall? Trees turn into an impressive array of colours in autumn as a result of the chlorophyll disappearing from their leaves. Chlorophyll is the pigment in trees that gives leaves their green colour, and it plays a vital role in photosynthesis, a process that turns light energy into

food (sugar) for the tree. As winter approaches, photosynthesis stops in deciduous trees because there is not enough available water or light, and chlorophyll disappears from the leaves. As the chlorophyll disappears, the other pigments already in the leaves become visible. Carotenoids, xanthophylls and anthocyanins are responsible for the brilliant yellow, orange, red, purple and crimson colours in the leaves.

The leaves of deciduous trees fall in autumn because a layer of cork develops between the leaf stem and the twig, which eventually kills the leaf.

Coniferous trees keep their needle-like leaves in winter thanks, in part, to a waxy covering that protects the leaves from losing too much water. One coniferous tree that does shed its leaves in the autumn is the tamarack, but not before putting on a stunning display as its needles turn from green to gold.

If you want to enjoy nature's autumn artistry closer to home, you can plant native trees with leaves that will change colour. Every autumn our family enjoys watching the maple trees along our driveway slowly transform from green to yellow and orange and then to red before falling to the ground. We also enjoy the tamarack tree at the end of our driveway as it goes from a lush green to a brilliant golden hue. Other trees around our property also turn to a variety of colours. Enjoying these colourful trees that change the appearance of the landscape daily is something we look forward to each autumn.

 websites: **www.parkreports.com/fall**
www.ontariotravel.net/publications/
fallcolourreport.pdf

The Bruce Trail

The long fight to save wild beauty represents democracy at its best.
It requires citizens to practice the hardest of virtues—self-restraint.

—Edwin Way Teale

AT A GLANCE

- The Bruce Trail connects many parks, conservation areas, nature reserves and other islands of wilderness as it winds its way from Queenston to Tobermory. The impressive trail acts as a backbone supporting a magnificent eco-corridor.

- The Niagara Escarpment was designated a UNESCO World Biosphere Reserve in 1990. This designation recognizes the escarpment as an internationally significant ecosystem, placing it with the likes of the Galapagos Islands and Africa's Serengeti, where species diversity is protected.

- The Bruce Trail is the oldest and longest continuous footpath in Canada.

- The Bruce Trail Conservancy has close to 900 kilometres of main trail and hundreds of kilometres of side trails. One of the organization's main goals is to permanently secure the nature corridor along the Niagara Escarpment.

Directions: The Bruce Trail has numerous access points.

 website: **www.brucetrail.org**

1

Running along the Niagara Escarpment from Queenston to Tobermory is the Bruce Trail—the oldest and longest continuous footpath in Canada. The Bruce Trail Conservancy's mission is to establish and maintain a conservation corridor along the Niagara Escarpment, protecting the scenic rocky ridge's ecosystems while promoting environmentally friendly access.

The Niagara Escarpment was designated a UNESCO World Biosphere Reserve in 1990. This designation recognizes the escarpment as an internationally significant ecosystem and places it with the likes of the Galapagos Islands and Africa's Serengeti, where species diversity is protected.

A small group of people recognized the Niagara Escarpment's ecological importance more than 30 years prior to it being designated a UNESCO World Biosphere Reserve. In 1959, Ray Lowes came up with the idea of a public trail that ran the entire length of the Niagara Escarpment.

The year 1960 saw the first meeting of the Bruce Trail Committee, and in 1962, Philip Gosling started to plan and blaze the trail. The Bruce Trail Association (renamed "The Bruce Trail Conservancy" in 2007) was incorporated in 1963, and

● *Bruce Trail near River Road in Mulmur Township*

regional clubs were established along the trail. The Bruce Trail Conservancy has nine member clubs, each of which manages a section of the Bruce Trail and is responsible for establishing, promoting and maintaining the trail in their area. The clubs are the Niagara Bruce Trail Club, the Iroquoia Bruce Trail Club, the Toronto Bruce Trail Club, the Caledon Hills Club, the Dufferin Hi-Land Bruce Trail Club, the Blue Mountains Bruce Trail Club, the Beaver Valley Bruce Trail Club, the Sydenham Bruce Trail Club and the Peninsula Bruce Trail Club.

In 1967, Canada's Centennial, the Bruce Trail officially opened. Today, the Bruce Trail Conservancy has close to 900 kilometres of main trail and hundreds of kilometres of side trails. Although much of the Bruce Trail has been secured, a major portion of the trail is still at risk of development. Purchasing land where the Bruce Trail goes allows the Bruce Trail Conservancy to permanently protect the ecosystems along the escarpment. These ecosystems include forests, streams, rivers, lakes, meadows, cliffs, marshes, swamps, bogs and fens.

The Niagara Escarpment itself was formed some 450 million years ago. The sedimentary rock ridge rises more than 500 metres above sea level in some parts and supports a wide variety of habitats. These habitats are home to an incredible number of plant and animal species—many of them rare.

We have already destroyed the majority of forests, wetlands and other natural habitats of southern Ontario. By securing land on the escarpment, the Bruce

Trail Conservancy is helping ensure that at least some of the natural environment will be saved. Old-growth eastern white cedar forests are found, and protected, on the escarpment's cliffs. These slow-growing trees are hundreds of years old, with the oldest being over 1000 years of age!

By protecting the land along the escarpment, the conservancy is also creating a long, unfragmented corridor of natural habitat. Habitat corridors result in increased immigration between areas, allowing for larger populations, less inbreeding, more foraging areas and increased species diversity. The Bruce Trail connects many parks, conservation areas, nature reserves and other islands of wilderness as it winds its way from Queenston to Tobermory. The impressive trail acts as a backbone supporting a magnificent eco-corridor.

If you plan on hiking the Bruce Trail or the parks, conservation areas and other wilderness spots on the Niagara Escarpment, you may want to obtain the latest edition of *The Bruce Trail Reference,* which contains trail descriptions and maps.

The Bruce Trail is a phenomenal footpath that provides hikers and nature enthusiasts with an invaluable opportunity to visit some of the most scenic areas in Ontario. Not only is the famous trail a joy to travel on, but it plays an even more important role, that of protecting natural habitat and biodiversity in an increasingly developed part of the province. Those who had the vision of this special wilderness corridor more than half a century ago, along

1

with those who have helped create and maintain this path and those who have donated to its upkeep and protection, are to be commended.

Our family has certainly encountered this footpath on the majority of our nature outings. Whether we were visiting Ball's Falls Conservation Area in the Niagara region, Spencer Gorge in the Hamilton area, Crawford Lake near Milton, Hockley Valley Provincial Nature Reserve northeast of Orangeville or the numerous waterfalls in Grey County, the Bruce Trail was there, or nearby, like an old friend.

We have also enjoyed visiting many areas of the Bruce Trail near our home in the northern part of Dufferin County in recent years. These scenic areas offer good hiking opportunities and breathtaking views in parts of the natural world that you never get tired of visiting.

● *Ferns are common in Rock Hill Corner.*

One of our favourite hikes is to the Bell Lookout in Mulmur Township between Horning's Mills and Terra Nova. We take the Bruce Trail north off River Road where the trail goes alongside the Pine River and the Pine River Fishing Pond, where the Bell Lookout Side Trail climbs steeply to the Bell Lookout. The Bell Lookout provides a lovely view across the Pine River Valley, which is particularly beautiful when the fall colours are at their peak.

Another hike we enjoy is the Bruce Trail's Boyne Valley Springs property. This scenic spot includes a creek, meadows and forests including Walker's Woods, a mature hardwood forest.

Close to this property is another fascinating spot: Rock Hill Corner. This spectacular area includes rock formations featuring cracks, crevices and even caves. Large eastern white cedars are common here, as are ferns and moss-covered rocks. It's not a large property, but you won't want to hurry through this scenic location, which reminds me more of a northern environment than a little area in Mulmur Township.

One property managed by the Bruce Trail Conservancy that we found by accident is the Cheltenham Badlands. Located on Olde Base Line Road west of Highway 10 near the villages of Inglewood and Cheltenham, this property is a good example of badlands topography.

Designated an Earth Science Area of Natural and Scientific Interest, the Cheltenham Badlands features Queenston Shale, a soft rock that is exposed to erosion in this region. In most areas in

Ontario where this shale is present, it is protected from erosion by overlying hard rock, sand or gravel. Poor farming practices, including overgrazing, in the early 1900s caused the shale to erode into ridges and gullies. The reddish colour of the Queenston Shale is a result of the iron oxide, and greenish bands are created by groundwater turning the red iron oxide to green iron oxide. These striking "badlands" are an important reminder of what can occur when we treat land poorly.

To help protect this environmentally sensitive site, please admire it from the flat area where the interpretive sign is located, and do not visit it when conditions are wet.

● *Cheltenham Badlands*

Woodend Conservation Area

The real value of nature is that people may enter it for a time, enjoy its beauty, its animals, and its plants, and return home renewed without having taken anything away from the environment.

—R. D. Lawrence

AT A GLANCE

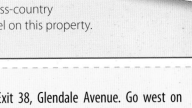

- In 1798, the United Empire Loyalist family of Peter Lampman settled what is now the Woodend Conservation Area, and Canadian poet Archibald Lampman visited and wrote about this property.

- The conservation area contains mature deciduous forest, including some Carolinian forest tree species.

- The grassy area and the mature forest are home to numerous species of plants and animals and provide good opportunities for hiking, picnics, birdwatching and nature appreciation. In the winter, cross-country skiing and snowshoeing are ways to travel on this property.

Directions: Take the QEW Niagara to Exit 38, Glendale Avenue. Go west on Glendale Avenue, turn south onto Taylor Road and proceed to the park entrance.

websites: **www.npca.ca**

www.npca.ca/conservation-areas/ woodend

2

Situated on top of the Niagara Escarpment in Niagara-on-the-Lake is the Woodend Conservation Area. This scenic 46-hectare property was acquired by the Niagara Peninsula Conservation Authority in 1974. In 1798, the United Empire Loyalist family of Peter Lampman settled what is now the Woodend Conservation Area, and Canadian poet Archibald Lampman—Peter Lampman's grandson—visited and wrote about this property.

The house on the property was originally built in the 1800s and was renovated in the early 1930s. Today the building serves as the Woodend Environmental Centre, an outdoor education facility operated by the District School Board of Niagara. Every year thousands of students learn about nature at this beautiful property.

The conservation area contains some open space as well as mature deciduous forest including some Carolinian forest tree species. Carolinian tree species found in the Woodend Conservation Area include sugar maple, American beech, red oak, shagbark hickory, rock elm, black cherry, black oak and pawpaw.

The property varies in elevation from 114 metres to more than 170 metres above sea level, and it contains a number of hiking trails, including a section of the Bruce Trail as well as the Hardwood Trail and the Silurian Adventure Trail. The Silurian Adventure Trail is approximately 1.5 kilometres long, and it runs through a deciduous forest and along the Niagara Escarpment edge. The grassy area and mature forest are home to numerous species of plants and animals and provide good opportunities for hiking, picnics, birdwatching and nature appreciation. In winter, cross-country skiing and snowshoeing are ways to travel on this property.

● *Woodend Environmental Centre*

We visited the Woodend Conservation Area during summer. We started off by admiring the grounds of the Woodend Environmental Centre, which features a beautiful house surrounded by mature native trees.

Next, we hiked the Silurian Adventure Trail. Beautiful trees exhibiting lush foliage and the amazing rock formations of the escarpment held our attention for the entire walk. The hike was an easy one that we didn't want to rush. The trees helped to minimize the noise from the busy Queen Elizabeth Way (QEW), which we could see in the distance, and provided us with relief from the sun and heat. Come fall, these trees will put on a show of brilliant colours, and when they shed their leaves, the views from the trail will be impressive.

Our leisurely stroll through the mature forest was relaxing and enjoyable. We also enjoyed the scenery of the escarpment, which Liam and Gleannan

● *Escarpment rock formations*

frequently took a closer look at where the rocky areas were safe to explore. Although our walk didn't take long to complete, it was one of the more pleasant walks I had experienced in a long time.

● *Liam explores rock formations next to the trail*

Ball's Falls Conservation Area

Conservation is a state of harmony between men and land.

—Aldo Leopold

AT A GLANCE

- Within the conservation area is a historical hamlet from the 19th century, including the Ball family's homestead, a gristmill and the ruins of a woollen mill.

- Ball's Falls Conservation Area has two waterfalls. The main Lower Falls are 27 metres high while the Upper Falls are 11 metres in height.

- Plant life in the Ball's Falls Conservation Area is diverse and includes more than 450 species of vascular plants and trees, including some Carolinian species.

Directions: Coming from Toronto, take the QEW Niagara and take Exit 57, Victoria Avenue. Turn right on South Service Road and then turn left on Victoria Avenue. Turn left on 6th Avenue and proceed to the park entrance.

 website: **www.ballsfalls.ca**

Located south of the village of Jordan, the Ball's Falls Conservation Area offers many activities for an educational and fun-filled day for the whole family. The Ball's Falls Centre for Conservation features temporary and permanent galleries pertaining to nature, conservation and culture.

Also within the conservation area is a historical hamlet from the 19th century, including the Ball family's second home and an 1807 gristmill. Other heritage buildings include a lime kiln, fruit drying shed, blacksmith shop, log cabin, carriage shed, barns and the ruins of a woollen mill. The well-maintained hamlet dates back to the early 1800s and is historically important because it contains the original buildings on their original site, along with the corresponding archival and artifact collection. The hamlet also includes a church that was built in 1864 and

was moved to the conservation area in 1974. These restored buildings are all that remain of the industrial hamlet that once featured mills, shops and homes, which were owned and rented by the Ball family.

Although the hamlet is a popular feature of the conservation area, for many visitors the two waterfalls, the Lower Falls and the Upper Falls, are the main attractions. Ball's Falls was named after John and George Ball. These brothers, in 1807, purchased 486 hectares of land along Twenty Mile Creek, including the two waterfalls. The site provided the Ball brothers with a source of power that enabled them to operate a gristmill, sawmill and woollen mill. The gristmill was in operation by 1809 and was important during the War of 1812, when it supplied flour to British regiments. The sawmill was built in 1816 at the edge of the Lower Falls, where it remained

● *The church was built in 1864.*

in operation until the early 1900s. In 1824, George Ball began construction of a five-storey woollen mill on a bluff along Twenty Mile Creek near the Upper Falls.

During the 1840s, George Ball's son, George Peter Mann Ball, built some houses and a boarding house to accommodate workers and residents. There were plans for the creation of a village, but unfortunately they were never realized largely as a result of the Great Western Railway bypassing the proposed industrial community in the early 1850s.

In 1962, Manley Ball, George Ball's great-grandson, sold what was left of the property, approximately 44.5 hectares, to the Niagara Peninsula Conservation Authority.

The Ball's Falls Conservation Area is now almost 113 hectares and has been designated an Historical Park; the bedrock gorge is a provincially significant

Earth Science Area of Natural and Scientific Interest (ANSI).

While the cultural history of the Ball's Falls Conservation Area is interesting, so too is the site's physical history. The area is located on the Niagara Escarpment, and some of its rock formations are more than 430 million years old. Glaciers retreated approximately 13,000 years ago, and the resulting meltwater created the gorges of Twenty Mile Creek. The Lower Falls are 27 metres high and the Upper Falls are 11 metres high. Originating in the City of Hamilton, Twenty Mile Creek flows through the towns of Grimsby and Lincoln before emptying into Lake Ontario. Water flow of the creek often dries up in late summer and fall.

Plant life in the Ball's Falls Conservation Area is diverse and includes more than 450 species of vascular plants and trees. Carolinian species in the conservation area include shagbark hickory, sassafras

● *Twenty Mile Creek*

and witch hazel. Forests of sugar maple, red oak, white oak and ironwood also grow here.

Many species of mammals, birds, amphibians, reptiles and fish can also be found in the park and its environs, including numerous threatened and rare species.

Following the banks of Twenty Mile Creek is the scenic Cataract Trail, which accesses the Upper Falls, the historical hamlet and the Lower Falls. The distances from the parking lot to the falls and back to the parking lot are approximately 1.3 kilometres for the Lower Falls and 1.7 kilometres for the Upper Falls.

There is no shortage of things to do at the Ball's Falls Conservation Area. You can hike to the two waterfalls, enjoy the natural surroundings, learn about conservation and life in a 19th-century hamlet or have a picnic. In winter you can snowshoe or cross-country ski on the area's ungroomed trails.

It was a warm August afternoon when we visited the Ball's Falls Conservation Area. After a quick visit to the Centre for Conservation, we took the Cataract Trail across Twenty Mile Creek. Much of the creek bed was dry because the region was experiencing a long, hot, dry period. I felt sorry for the fish who had gathered in some of the isolated, deeper pools. A short walk brought us into the hamlet, where we enjoyed visiting the buildings, including a fruit-drying shed and the beautiful red brick Ball homestead.

We were not too optimistic about seeing a lot of water flowing over the Lower Falls after seeing the dry state of

● *Cataract Trail*

Twenty Mile Creek. It was a good thing that our expectations were not high—there was barely a trickle coming over the falls. Although the lack of water was a little disappointing, it provided us with a good opportunity to observe the incredible rock formations.

The Cataract Trail took us back through the historical hamlet, where it followed the banks of Twenty Mile Creek towards the Upper Falls. Not far from the Upper Falls we came across the ruins of the five-storey woollen mill. An interpretive sign at the site provides information about this once-impressive structure including a photograph of the mill in 1880. Not much of the building is left except part of a wall.

After checking out the mill ruins, we proceeded along the trail to the Upper Falls. As with the Lower Falls, the Upper Falls were mostly dry. In fact, the creek bed at the top of the falls was dry. Some water flowed under-ground, emerging part way down the cliffs and forming a pool at the base of the waterfall. The dry conditions allowed us to observe the creek bed. Even though there was little water, the view down the gorge was spectacular. We were in no hurry to leave this scenic spot, and after lingering here for a while we enjoyed a leisurely hike back to the parking lot.

● *Upper Falls*

3

● *Ruins of woollen mill*

Beamer Memorial Conservation Area

*The air up there in the clouds is very pure and fine, bracing and delicious.
And why shouldn't it be?—it is the same the angels breathe.*

—Mark Twain

AT A GLANCE

- Beamer Memorial Conservation Area is recognized as one of the best places in the Niagara Peninsula to observe the annual hawk migration.

- The two waterfalls in Beamer Memorial Conservation Area, Upper Beamer Falls and Lower Beamer Falls, are both approximately 6 metres in height.

- The Lookout Trail takes you to several lookout points with impressive views of Grimsby, the Niagara Escarpment and Lake Ontario as well as the Forty Mile Creek Valley.

Directions: On the QEW to Grimsby take the Christie Street exit. Go south on Christie Street, which turns into Mountain Road. Take Mountain Road up the escarpment and go west on Ridge Road to Quarry Road and to the conservation area entrance. There is also a small, unmarked parking area on your right as you are travelling west on Ridge Road. This parking area is near the falls.

 websites: **www.npca.ca**

**www.npca.ca/conservation-areas/
beamer-memorial**

On the edge of the Niagara Escarpment overlooking the town of Grimsby sits the Beamer Memorial Conservation Area. The picturesque 55-hectare property was acquired by the Niagara Peninsula Conservation Authority in 1964.

In 1790, John and Anna Beamer settled this land, where they built a sawmill that was powered by the Forty Mile Creek. The gorge of Forty Mile Creek was created by meltwater when the last glaciers retreated approximately 13,000 years ago. There are two waterfalls on the creek, Upper Beamer Falls and Lower Beamer Falls, both of which are approximately 6 metres in height.

While the two waterfalls and the Forty Mile Creek Valley are popular features of the Beamer Memorial Conservation Area, its location has resulted in it being designated as an Important Bird Area (IBA). In fact, it may be most recognized as the best place

in the Niagara Peninsula to observe the annual hawk migration, which sees tens of thousands of hawks along with eagles, falcons and vultures following the shorelines of Lake Ontario and Lake Erie as they migrate north. Every spring since 1975, from March to May, people have gathered here to watch the migration of birds of prey as they fly north to their breeding grounds. Some of the species migrating include red-tailed hawks, sharp-shinned hawks, bald eagles, peregrine falcons and turkey vultures. On a good day over 1000 raptors can be counted!

Birds of prey migrate during the day and rely on updrafts that allow them to soar and glide. Winds coming off the lake and contacting the cliffs, combined with fields heating up during the day, provide hawks and other raptors with strong thermal updrafts that they can glide on while conserving energy for their long migration.

red-tailed hawk

The Beamer Memorial Conservation Area is also an Area of Natural and Scientific Interest (ANSI). The Bruce Trail, along with the Bruce Side Trail and the Lookout Trail, take you to scenic areas. The Lookout Trail leads to several lookout points that provide impressive views of Grimsby, the Niagara Escarpment and Lake Ontario as well as the Forty Mile Creek Valley.

The trails also take you through mature Carolinian forest containing sugar maple, red oak and other deciduous trees. Eastern white cedar trees are common along the escarpment.

bald eagle

Over 300 species of plants are found in the conservation area including many species of wildflowers.

The trails in the Beamer Memorial Conservation Area go close to the edge of the escarpment, so exercise caution when hiking. It is also important to stay on the marked trails, as this conservation area features steep slopes and sensitive habitat that can easily be damaged.

It was an early August evening when Lynn, Liam, Gleannan and I visited the Beamer Memorial Conservation Area. We took the Lookout Trail into the conservation area, and the path through a mature deciduous forest made for an enjoyable walk. Soon we came to a lookout with a beautiful view of Grimsby immediately below us followed by Lake Ontario and, because it was a fairly clear day, the Toronto skyline in the distance. Other lookouts provided spectacular views of the Niagara Escarpment.

As we followed the Lookout Trail, we enjoyed the scenic footpath that ran next to the escarpment and through a mature deciduous forest that shielded us from the sun. We were very careful on sections of the trail that were literally a part of the edge of the escarpment and where eastern white cedars cling to rock cliffs.

After leaving the main parking lot on Quarry Road, we drove to another unmarked parking area within the park on Ridge Road, where we were able to observe Upper Beamer Falls on Forty Mile Creek. There wasn't a lot of water going over the falls, so we had the opportunity to observe the gorge in a relatively dry state. The view of the scenic gorge of Forty Mile Creek as the water gently flowed over the rocks along the creek made for a wonderful place to rest and relax after a day of hiking. The sound of the water spilling over the rocks and creating miniature waterfalls along the creek was pleasant.

Although summer is an enjoyable time to visit this conservation area, we plan on returning during spring when we can watch the birds of prey. In spring, there should also be more water going over the waterfalls. Autumn will also be a good time to visit the area because the colours will be spectacular from the lookout areas.

4

- *Lookout Trail*

Tiffany Falls Conservation Area

We abuse land because we regard it as a commodity belonging to us. When we see land as a community to which we belong, we may begin to use it with love and respect. There is no other way for land to survive the impact of mechanized man, nor for us to reap from it the aesthetic harvest it is capable, under science, of contributing to culture.

—Aldo Leopold

AT A GLANCE

5

- More than 200 species of vascular plants have been recorded in and around the conservation area, along with numerous species of butterflies and breeding birds, including Carolinian bird species, such as the Louisiana waterthrush and the tufted titmouse.

- The Tiffany Falls Access Trail takes you along a creek and forested valley to the 21-metre high waterfall.

- The falls were named after Dr. Oliver Tiffany, who was the first known physician in the Ancaster area.

Directions: From the east, take Highway 403 into Hamilton to the Rousseaux Street exit. Take Rousseaux Street to Wilson Street and turn east, then proceed to the parking lot on the south side of Wilson Street.

From the west, take Highway 403 to the Wilson Street exit and proceed east on Wilson Street past Rousseaux Street. Continue to the parking lot on the south side of Wilson Street.

websites: **www.conservationhamilton.ca**

http://waterfalls.hamilton.ca

Tiffany Falls Conservation Area is a small piece of wilderness in an urbanized area. It is a scenic spot in the community of Ancaster in Hamilton that links to other nearby natural areas, providing important habitat for species and a corridor for them to travel through. This natural area connects to the wilderness areas of the Dundas Valley. The 7-hectare property is managed by the Hamilton Region Conservation Authority and is a Significant Natural Area and a Regional Earth Science Area of Natural and Scientific Interest (ANSI).

The waterfall was named after Dr. Oliver Tiffany, the first known physician in the Ancaster area. Dr. Tiffany began his practice between 1796 and 1798, where he worked for more than 40 years until his death in 1835. The scenic Tiffany Creek, which is a tributary stream in the Spencer Creek system, and Tiffany Falls were part of Dr. Tiffany's property.

The parking lot for this conservation area is on Wilson Street. The Tiffany Falls Access Trail, an approximately 400-metre side trail of the Bruce Trail, takes you to the 21-metre-high waterfall. The easy, scenic trail runs along the creek and the forested valley, which features steep talus slopes. Two footbridges over the creek and a lookout near the falls complement the footpath.

During dry periods, little water flows over the falls and the creek is also fairly dry, with only pools of water. Even during times of low water levels, the creek,

5

- *Tiffany Falls access trail*

forested valley and waterfall are beautiful and definitely worth a visit. The main Bruce Trail goes through the area and accesses nearby Sherman Falls.

For safety reasons and to protect this environmentally sensitive area, it is important to stay on the trail (which you should always do anyway), and do not climb the talus slopes around Tiffany Falls or along the creek valley.

Besides preserving the beauty of this valley, including the creek and waterfall, Tiffany Creek Conservation Area is important in that it provides a haven for animals and native plants in an otherwise overly developed area. It also links the greenbelt of the Niagara Escarpment to natural areas in Dundas Valley. These eco-corridors are crucial for animals as well as for maintaining species diversity.

There are some rare and endangered species in and around the Tiffany Falls Conservation Area, which contains interior forest habitat. More than 200 species of vascular plants have been recorded in the area along with numerous species of butterflies and breeding birds.

This Environmentally Significant Area provides habitat for Carolinian bird species, such as the Louisiana waterthrush and the tufted titmouse. The Louisiana waterthrush is a federal Species of Concern in Canada; its habitat includes forested ravines that contain tumbling waters and moss-covered rocks. The tufted titmouse is a permanent resident and prefers deciduous forest habitat—like that found at Tiffany Falls Conservation Area. This species of bird is rare in Ontario.

Common trees in the V-shaped ravine with talus slopes include sugar maple, black maple, eastern hemlock and white ash. The area is also home to the endangered butternut.

5

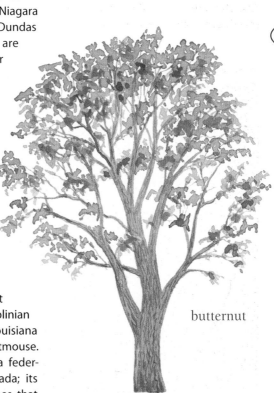

butternut

We arrived at Tiffany Falls Conservation Area on an early summer evening after a day of hiking. This small conservation area with its short trail is an ideal spot for tired hikers who have not yet had their day's fill of nature.

It was a short hike from the parking lot to Tiffany Falls, and the trail was in good shape and easy to walk. The Tiffany Creek valley was beautiful; the lush forest and steep valley slopes that descend to the stream provided a wonderful scene and a glimpse of how much of the area

● *Gleannan reading an interpretive sign about Tiffany Falls*

would have looked many years ago before "progress" took over.

There wasn't a lot of water in Tiffany Creek, but the meandering stream that flowed and gurgled over rocks as it made its way through the mostly deciduous forest was a joy to watch. The trail is never far from the creek, and the two footbridges provided nice views up and down the valley. We stopped on these bridges to fully appreciate this exceptional wilderness area in the middle of a large, urban centre. Many of the trees were quite old, and moss-covered rocks were everywhere. Wildflowers and other plants were common and added to the lush, green environment. Looking at the plants and trees along Tiffany Creek, you wouldn't have thought that we were experiencing a long, hot, dry period.

Although there wasn't much water in Tiffany Creek or flowing over the falls, the scene as we approached Tiffany Falls was impressive. Enough water flowed over the falls to make the sights and sounds interesting, while allowing you to clearly see the rock formations and the vegetation clinging to them. Trees were growing next to the creek above the falls as well as on the steep slope next to the waterfall.

The lookout near the bottom of Tiffany Falls has interpretive signs informing visitors about the falls, creek and some of the resident species. This is also a good location from which to take photographs. Although the falls will capture your attention, take the time to enjoy the view downstream through the valley as well.

After relaxing and taking in the beauty around the falls, we followed the trail back to the parking lot. This nature outing only took us about 35 minutes, but Tiffany Falls was definitely worth visiting.

● *Tiffany Creek and valley*

Spencer Gorge/Webster's Falls Conservation Area

People might no longer believe much in the old concepts of heaven—clouds you can walk on, stringed instruments you can finally play—but they do believe, more and more, in finding pieces of heaven here on earth.

—Roy MacGregor

AT A GLANCE

- Spencer Gorge/Webster's Falls Conservation Area has many scenic features including two waterfalls, gorges, creeks, forests, the Bruce Trail and picnic areas.

- The two waterfalls are Webster's Falls and Tew's Falls. Webster's Falls is 22 metres high while Tew's Falls is 41 metres high—just a few metres less than Niagara Falls.

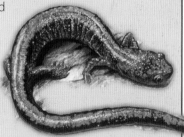

- Numerous species of fish, reptiles and amphibians, such as the red-backed salamander, also reside in and around the Spencer Gorge.

6

Directions: From Highway 401 go south on Highway 6 to Highway 5 (Dundas Street) and turn west. Turn south on Brock Road and proceed to Harvest Road. Watch for signs for Tew's Falls. For Webster's Falls, turn east on Harvest Road and go to Short Road, then turn south. Short Road curves into Fallsview Road. Watch for signs for Webster's Falls.

websites: **www.conservationhamilton.ca**

http://waterfalls.hamilton.ca

■ A nice location to enjoy nature, maybe have a picnic or take a hike, is the Spencer Gorge/Webster's Falls Conservation Area. Located in the community of Greensville in Hamilton, this area has many scenic features including two waterfalls, gorges, creeks, forests, the Bruce Trail and picnic areas. This conservation area was one of the more popular spots that we came across, and photography is a common activity here. Besides the beautiful natural areas, there are landscaped, grassy expanses that are suitable for playing or having a picnic.

The two waterfalls in this conservation area are Webster's Falls and Tew's Falls. Webster's Falls was originally known as Dr. Hamilton's Falls, because Dr. James Hamilton bought the property in 1818. A year later, the waterfall and the 31.5 hectares were purchased by Joseph Webster Sr. after he and his family arrived from England. Around 1830, Joseph Webster Sr.'s son, Joseph Jr., rebuilt a distillery and a gristmill on the property, which were enlarged in 1842, and an oatmeal and barley mill were also added. George W. Harper and W.S. Merrill purchased the mills in 1891 and expanded them, but these buildings were lost to fire in 1898. In 1899 a power house was built at the foot of Webster's Falls, which supplied electricity to the local community, but it was destroyed by fire in 1901.

In 1933, the grounds around Webster's Falls were landscaped and a cobblestone bridge was constructed across the creek above the falls. The Hamilton Conservation Authority acquired the property in 2000.

● Webster's Falls

6

● Sign at Webster's Falls

The rock of Webster's Falls and Tew's Falls began to form approximately 450 million years ago when sedimentary material started to accumulate. This build-up of material continued for about 150 million years. Approximately 10,000 years ago, glacial meltwaters carved the gorges around these falls that we see today.

Webster's Falls is 22 metres high and is fed by Spencer Creek; Tew's Falls is 41 metres high, just a few metres less than Niagara Falls, and is fed by Logie's Creek. The area around these waterfalls and Spencer Gorge has been designated a Significant Natural Area as well as a Life Science Area of Natural and Scientific Interest (ANSI) and an Earth Science Area of Natural and Scientific Interest (ANSI). It provides habitat for many species, including rare and endangered species.

The diverse habitats of the conservation area and its environs are home to more than 500 species of plants that are found in the mature forests and on the talus slopes and cliffs—including many rare species such as red mulberry, yellow mandarin and American chestnut. As with much of the Niagara Escarpment, eastern white cedars grow on steep cliffs where their roots gain a hold in crevices in search of water and nutrients. Because these trees live in such harsh conditions, they grow slowly, but many are very old despite their younger appearance. Two cedars growing side by side on the cliffs next to Webster's Falls are more than 500 years old. These would have been young

● *Stairs leading to Webster's Falls*

trees when Jacques Cartier sailed up the St. Lawrence River in the 1530s.

The variety of habitats results in a diversity of animal species including many species of birds such as the rare Louisiana waterthrush, flycatchers and sparrows. Numerous species of fish, reptiles and amphibians, such as the red-backed salamander, also reside in and around the Spencer Gorge.

Louisiana waterthrush

A good way to see Webster's Falls and Tew's Falls is by hiking the Bruce Trail. It is less than a kilometre from Webster's Falls to Tew's Falls. Hiking 1.3 kilometres past Tew's Falls will take you to the Dundas

Peak, where you will enjoy nice views of Dundas and Hamilton.

It was almost evening in early August when our family arrived at the Spencer Gorge/Webster's Falls Conservation Area. Even though it was late in the day, many people were admiring the falls, having a picnic or playing on the manicured lawns. It was a short walk from the parking lot over to a viewing area with an attractive stone fence. After spending some time looking at the Webster's Falls and the Spencer Gorge, we walked farther along the trail to get a different view. These falls and the gorge really are spectacular. I can only imagine how the area looks in spring or fall, when larger volumes of water flow over the cliffs onto the massive boulders below. The cobblestone bridge over Spencer Creek above the

6

● *Cobblestone bridge across Spencer Creek above Webster's falls*

falls added to the scenic sight. We hiked a short way down the trail that went through a beautiful, mature deciduous forest, and then we explored some of the landscaped areas above the waterfall.

Because we were short on time but wanted to see Tew's Falls, we drove the short distance along Harvest Road to a smaller parking lot for Tew's Falls where the waterfall is located approximately 150 metres from the parking lot. We lingered at the viewing area for some time, watching the water from Logie's Creek spill over the edge of the rock cliff and crash onto the rocks below. Mature deciduous forests surround this waterfall making for a particularly attractive, natural setting. On the way back to the parking lot, we stopped at a small wetland area where we took photographs of a monarch butterfly. We also wanted to see Dundas Peak, but because of a lack of time that hike will have to wait for another time.

● *Monarch butterfly near Tew's Falls*

6

Rattray Marsh Conservation Area

Hope and the future for me are not in lawns and cultivated fields, not in towns and cities, but in the impervious and quaking swamps.

—Henry David Thoreau

AT A GLANCE

- Rattray Marsh Conservation Area is a 38-hectare wetland in the Greater Toronto Area.

- It provides critical habitat for wetland birds in an urban environment and is an important stopover area for migrating waterfowl and other birds.

- More than 20 species of fish have been found in Rattray Marsh, which is an important spawning habitat for northern pike.

- The marsh was formed at the mouth of Sheridan Creek where it enters Lake Ontario.

7

Directions: In Mississauga, take Lakeshore Road West to Jack Darling Memorial Park (1180 Lakeshore Road West) and walk west on the Waterfront Trail into Rattray Marsh Conservation Area.

 website: **www.creditvalleyca.ca**

Although people are slowly becoming enlightened as to the importance of wetlands, our past ignorance has resulted in the vast majority of these ecosystems being eliminated from southern Ontario. Fortunately, dedicated individuals and groups of people have worked to protect some of the remaining wetland habitat, and Rattray Marsh is one such place.

Located in the Clarkson area of Mississauga on Lake Ontario, and fed by Sheridan Creek as well as from springs and Lake Ontario, Rattray Marsh Conservation Area is a 38-hectare wetland ecosystem in the Greater Toronto Area. The conservation area was the property of Colonel James Rattray, who lived in the Barrymede mansion on this stunning property from 1916 until 1945. Prior to his death in 1959, he attempted to have the government take over this lagoon, which was created when glaciers retreated. Colonel Rattray's efforts were taken over by various others following his death, and in 1972 Credit Valley Conservation secured this wetland. Unfortunately, some development occurred before the organization obtained the property.

In 1975, the Rattray Marsh Conservation Area was officially opened, and in 1979 the Rattray Marsh Protection Association was formed. This volunteer group protects the marsh with its stewardship and education initiatives. Rattray Marsh has been given various designations including a Natural Area, an Environmentally Significant Area, a Provincially Significant Wetland and Wildlife Habitat and a Life Science Area of Natural and Scientific Interest (ANSI).

Within the conservation area are various habitats including beach, marsh, swamp, meadow and upland forest. As you would expect, this productive and diverse ecosystem is home to a variety of plant and animal life. Approximately 450 plant species have been recorded here, including Carolinian species such as black oak, shagbark hickory, sassafras and witch-hazel.

Birds are also well represented at this wetland—more than 220 species have been recorded, including the Caspian tern, the great egret, other herons, plovers and sandpipers. Not only does this marsh provide critical habitat for wetland birds in an otherwise urban environment, but it is also an important stopover area for migrating waterfowl and other birds.

Trail into Rattray Marsh from the Waterfront Trail

7

● *Upland Forest*

Besides birds, the marsh is home to many other animals such as frogs, snakes and turtles, including the provincially rare northern map turtle and the eastern milk snake which is a Species of Concern. Rattray Marsh is also an important hibernation area for the snapping turtle.

More than 20 species of fish have been found in Rattray Marsh, which is an important spawning habitat for northern pike. Sheridan Creek is an important spawning area for the white sucker.

More than 20 species of mammals have also been recorded in the marsh.

Birdwatching, nature appreciation, photography and hiking are popular activities at Rattray Marsh, and interpretive signs inform visitors about this marsh and wetlands in general.

Rattray Marsh was formed at the mouth of Sheridan Creek where it enters Lake Ontario. A baymouth bar, including a rare cobble beach, separates the marsh from Lake Ontario. Marsh water levels are controlled both by the water level in the lake and the flow in Sheridan Creek. Over thousands of years, storms from Lake Ontario have deposited smooth, flat rocks where the marsh meets the lake, forming a shingle bar. This bar stopped, or slowed, the water from Sheridan Creek

7

caspian tern

making its way to Lake Ontario, thus creating Rattray Marsh. Sections of the shingle bar can be washed out when water levels in Sheridan Creek are raised; the damaging and building up of the shingle bar is an ongoing process. The Sheridan Creek watershed drains more than 1000 hectares.

Unfortunately, Rattray Marsh is being affected in many ways. Surrounded by urban development and paved surfaces, this environmentally sensitive ecosystem is susceptible to significant surface water runoff, pollution and sediments carried in the runoff. The runoff also carries excess nutrients from the surrounding area, which causes eutrophication and reduces vegetation diversity. Non-native species also affect ecosystems, and Rattray Marsh is no exception. Common carp and purple

loosestrife are two alien species that adversely affect the marsh. There are plans to restore the depth of the marsh by removing mineral soils that have accumulated on top of the original organic deposits, which will help bring back native vegetation as well as animals. There are also plans to prevent, or minimize, the impacts of carp on the ecosystem.

A trail has been created to help protect this sensitive wetland while encouraging people to visit and enjoy the marsh. The trail includes a raised boardwalk to keep visitors on the trails and away from the more fragile areas of the marsh. There are also three viewing platforms. Staying on the trails is particularly important in Rattray Marsh, and fishing, cycling and motorized vehicles are prohibited in this wetland sanctuary. Dogs must be kept on a leash at all times.

● *Boardwalk in the conservation area*

Lynn and I visited Rattray Marsh at the end of August. We parked our car at Jack Darling Memorial Park in the morning and hiked the short distance, approximately 500 metres, west along the Waterfront Trail past Turtle Creek and into Rattray Marsh.

The views along Lake Ontario were impressive. The trails are easy to walk and access a variety of habitats. Marsh vegetation at the end of August was both lush and green and many plants along the trails were in bloom. The upland forests were beautiful and featured many old trees.

7

● *Chicory* ● *Spotted touch-me-not* ● *Dogwood*

While hiking the trails we saw numerous species of birds in the marsh including gulls, mallards and a great egret. After walking through the forests and wetland areas, we checked out the barrier beach that consists of smooth, flat rocks pushed onto the shore during storms on Lake Ontario.

Just off the barrier beach in Lake Ontario were numerous birds including a family of mute swans. Although mute swans are not a native species,

the sight of these and other birds on Lake Ontario with Toronto's skyline in the background while waves lapped against the shore was most enjoyable. Lynn and I stayed here for some time before heading back to Jack Darling Memorial Park.

Our visit to Rattray Marsh lasted a few hours. This important wetland is beautiful throughout the year, and we plan on a return visit in spring when even more birds will be present.

● *Family of mute swans on Lake Ontario near the marsh*

7

CRAWFORD LAKE

CONSERVATION HALTON

Iroquoian
Village

Turtle Island Festival
Coming this fall
conservationhalton.ca

Crawford Lake Conservation Area

Perhaps nature is our best assurance of immortality.

—Eleanor Roosevelt

AT A GLANCE

- Crawford Lake Conservation Area is 232 hectares in size and features a meromictic lake and a reconstructed 15th-century Iroquoian village.

- The Iroquoian village was reconstructed on its original site using archaeological research, written records from Jesuit missionaries and early explorers as well as information provided by First Nations communities and Elders.

- Created approximately 12,000 years ago when glaciers retreated from this area, Crawford Lake is fed by springs. The Crawford Lake Trail is a 1.4-kilometre trail consisting of an elevated boardwalk around the lake.

- The natural and cultural heritage features found at the Crawford Lake Conservation Area make it a good place for educational opportunities, and tens of thousands of students visit this conservation area annually.

8

Directions: Take Highway 401 to the Guelph Line and go south to Conservation Road (formerly Steeles Avenue) and turn east to the park entrance.

 website: **www.conservationhalton.ca**

Located on the Niagara Escarpment near the community of Campbellville in Milton, is Crawford Lake Conservation Area. This natural environmental park, owned and managed by Conservation Halton, is 232 hectares in size and features a meromictic lake and a 15th-century reconstructed Iroquoian village. The area has more than 12 kilometres of trails consisting of overlapping loops. This park has been designated an Area of Natural and Scientific Interest (ANSI), a Provincially Significant Wetland and an Environmentally Sensitive Area.

Although there is a lot to see and do at this popular conservation area, the lake itself is the main attraction. Created approximately 12,000 years ago when glaciers retreated from the area, the lake is fed by springs, and water flows from the lake through a swamp and into a tributary of Bronte Creek. The lake has a relatively small surface area but has a depth of over 24 metres.

Crawford Lake is a rare kind of lake known as a meromictic lake. This type of lake is uncommon in Canada—there are only approximately 30 other known ones in the country. Meromictic lakes are permanently stratified. Usually water in lakes in the temperate zone completely mix in spring and fall, when water temperatures at the top and the bottom of the lake are almost the same. One of the reasons why a lake doesn't mix in such a manner is that water in deeper lakes can't be mixed by wind energy. Crawford Lake is a deep lake with a small surface area. It is also protected from the wind by cliffs and forests, so there is little wave action to

● *Crawford Lake is surrounded by cedar trees.*

8

circulate the water, leaving the very cold water at the bottom of the lake.

With limited circulation and little oxygen found below 15 metres in Crawford Lake, little life is evident there and little decomposition occurs. Whatever sinks to the bottom of the lake, such as pollen, is preserved; there is nothing to break it down. As a result, the sediment on the bottom of Crawford Lake is a time capsule of sorts—the annual light and dark bands of sediment, called varves, reveal an historical record of human activity and vegetation changes. A sedimentation study in 1971 was instrumental in the discovery of a nearby Iroquoian Village in 1973.

The 15th-century Iroquoian Village was reconstructed on its original site using archaeological research, written records from Jesuit missionaries and early explorers as well as information provided by First Nations communities and Elders. The reconstructed village contains longhouses, a palisade, the Three Sisters Garden, a central fire pit, a games field and more. It is estimated that 250 people lived in the village, which had five longhouses.

More recent history on this site involves the Crawford family. George Crawford purchased approximately 40 hectares around the lake, then named Little Lake, in 1883. Two years later he sold

● *Turtle Clan longhouse*

8

the property to his son Murray. In 1898, Murray entered into an agreement with Richard Corrigan to protect the lake, which was renamed Crawford Lake, and they formed the Crawford Lake Company. In 1969, Lloyd Crawford, son of Murray and grandson of George, sold Crawford Lake and the land around it to the Halton Region Conservation Authority, which is now Conservation Halton.

One legend associated with Crawford Lake involves workmen and a team of horses who were cutting ice out of the frozen lake. Unfortunately, the ice broke and the cutting equipment pulled the horses down to the bottom of Crawford Lake. As a result of the special nature of

● *Boardwalk around Crawford Lake*

8

the lake, if the horses did indeed meet such a fate, they would still be preserved on the lake bottom. Interpretive staff can elaborate on this tragic, but fascinating, piece of the park's oral tradition if you want to hear more about the story.

Crawford Lake Conservation Area, also has a good network of hiking trails, including some that are designated for cross-country skiing and snowshoeing during winter. The Crawford Lake Trail is a popular 1.4-kilometre trail consisting of an elevated boardwalk around the lake. The boardwalk protects the environmentally sensitive shoreline, so it is important to stay on the wooden footpath. Interpretive signs provide intriguing information about the lake.

The Woodland Trail is 1.5 kilometres long and accesses forests and wetlands, and the Pine Ridge Trail is 3.6 kilometres long and goes through woodlands and meadows. Other trails include the Escarpment Trail (2.4 kilometres), the Snowshoe Trail (3.4 kilometres), a section of the Bruce Trail and the Nassagaweya Trail, a linear 7.2-kilometre trail that goes from Crawford Lake Conservation Area to Rattlesnake Point Conservation Area.

The variety of habitats found in the conservation area provide homes for many plants and animals including many rare and uncommon species. More than 600 plant species, including some eastern white cedars, 123 bird species, 33 species of mammals, 13 reptile species and 9 species of amphibians have been recorded in the conservation area and its environs.

The natural and cultural heritage features found at the Crawford Lake Conservation Area make it a good place for educational opportunities, and tens of thousands of students visit this conservation area annually.

It was late in the afternoon in August when Lynn, Liam, Gleannan and I arrived at Crawford Lake. We were all looking forward to seeing the meromictic lake, and we weren't disappointed. The short hike through the unique sugar maple bedrock forest down to the lake was enjoyable. The view from the north end of Crawford Lake was beautiful. Stepping onto the boardwalk was the beginning of an approximately half-hour hike that took us around the entire lake. Besides the stunning scenery of the lake, woods and rocks, the interpretive signs about the lake, the Iroquoians and the Crawfords also attracted our attention.

After hiking around Crawford Lake, we strolled over to the reconstructed Iroquoian Village. We were in time to hear an informative talk about what life in the village would have been like 500 years ago. Not only was the presentation interesting, but the atmosphere was also very good as it was held in the dimly lit Turtle Clan longhouse.

Although we could have spent considerably more time at the Crawford Lake Conservation Area, it was already evening so we left further explorations for another day.

8

Rattlesnake Point Conservation Area

...wildness is of inherent worth. It is sacred. It is the essence of who we are as Canadians and of this great northern wilderness called Canada. In destroying it, we destroy our soul.

—Rick Searle

AT A GLANCE

- This 294-hectare park is situated on the Milton Outlier—a section of the Niagara Escarpment that is separated from the main section by the Nassagaweya Canyon.

- Numerous old-growth eastern white cedars are in the conservation area. Growing in harsh conditions, many of these trees are considerably older than they appear, and one of the trees is approximately 600 years old.

- Complementing a good trail system in the park are five lookouts that offer stunning views of the surrounding countryside.

Directions: From Highway 401, take Highway 25 south to Steeles Avenue. Go west on Steeles Avenue to Appleby Line, and then south on Appleby to the park entrance.

9

 website: **www.conservationhalton.ca**

If you like spectacular views, impressive cliffs, beautiful forests and good hiking trails, you will enjoy Rattlesnake Point Conservation Area. Situated on the Milton Outlier—a section of the Niagara Escarpment that is separated from the main section by the Nassagaweya Canyon—in Milton, this 294-hectare park was established in 1961. The conservation area has a rich diversity of habitats and has been designated as an Environmentally Sensitive Area and an Area of Natural and Scientific Interest (ANSI).

Close to 600 plant species, 50 bird species, 11 mammal species, 18 species of fish, 5 reptile species and 7 amphibian species have been recorded in Rattlesnake Point and the surrounding area. Many of the species are rare or uncommon.

● *Eastern white cedars growing on rocks*

9

Numerous old-growth eastern white cedars are also in the conservation area. Growing in harsh conditions, many of these trees are considerably older than they appear, and one of the trees is approximately 600 years old! This tree started life around the same time that Joan of Arc did. These ancient trees need protecting, so admire them from a distance to be sure you don't damage their branches or their roots.

Rattlesnake Point Conservation Area also features limestone cliffs that were formed more than 400 million years ago when a tropical sea covered this area. Because the cliffs vary in height from 10 to 25 metres, it is vital that you do not get too close to the edges and that you do not climb over the lookout walls. Dogs must be on a leash and children need to be supervised so that they can't get into a dangerous situation. To protect the environmentally sensitive area, and to help ensure your safety, it is important to stay on the marked trails.

The trail system in the conservation area is good. A network of footpaths, including several loop trails and the Bruce Trail, result in more than 10 kilometres of cliff edge and forest trails. There are also numerous group campsites. If you are up for a longer hike, the Nassagaweya Trail connects the Rattlesnake Point and Crawford Lake conservation areas.

Complementing the trail system are five lookouts that offer stunning views of the surrounding countryside. The Trafalgar Lookout has a view of Lake Ontario and Toronto, and the

Nelson Lookout provides a view of the Lowville area and Mount Nemo. In between these lookouts is the Pinnacle Lookout. Set among the rocks, stairs at the Pinnacle Lookout take you to areas where you can view the cliffs, talus slopes and trees more closely. These stairs allow you to access areas that you normally wouldn't be able to reach. For views of the valley between Rattlesnake Point and Crawford Lake, go to the Buffalo Crag Lookout and the Nassagaweya Lookout.

Besides the impressive cliffs, this conservation area also contains forested and talus slopes, natural springs that feed into Bronte Creek, and the headwaters of Limestone Creek. Hardwood forests, valleys and fields are also found in the park.

Hiking and nature appreciation are popular activities in this wilderness area, as are picnicking, photography and group camping.

In an area that is being developed at an alarming rate, it is somewhat reassuring to know that there are still natural areas where people can go to get rejuvenated and enjoy a beautiful wilderness area in south-central Ontario. This oasis in a rapidly growing sea of urbanization is also vital for the animals who live here and for maintaining species diversity. The fact that this piece of wilderness is connected to other natural areas, such as the Crawford Lake Conservation Area, means that there are still corridors of wilderness where animals and plants can travel. As urbanization encroaches on rural areas, it is imperative that these pieces of nature are protected and allowed to grow.

It was mid-afternoon on a sunny summer day when Lynn, Liam, Gleannan and I arrived at Rattlesnake Point Conservation Area. Walking the trails through the deciduous forest to some of the lookouts was enjoyable, and the forest's protective canopy shielded us from the hot sun.

Close to the lookouts, at the rocky areas of the escarpment, eastern white cedars were common and their incredible root systems spread out among the rocks and limited soil. The lookouts provided amazing views across the countryside.

It is always nice to leave something for another day, and hiking the Nassagaweya Trail from Rattlesnake Point to Crawford Lake is something we are looking forward to.

● *The stairs allow good views of the cliffs*

9

Fletcher Creek Ecological Preserve

True wisdom consists in not departing from nature and in molding our conduct according to her laws and model.

—Seneca

AT A GLANCE

- Part of the Fletcher Creek Ecological Preserve includes the rehabilitation of an old quarry. Limestone was mined in this area and the quarry was abandoned in the 1930s.

- The abandoned quarry was transformed into a calcareous fen. Species diversity in this type of ecosystem is unusually high.

- An approximately 3-kilometre trail system allows the hiker access to old fields, cedar forests, Fletcher Creek and the old quarry ponds.

Directions: Take Highway 401 to Highway 6 and go south for approximately 6 kilometres to Flamborough Concession 11 W (Gore Road). Go west on Flamborough Concession 11 W for a little over 4 kilometres to Concession 7, then go north on Concession 7 for a few hundred metres to the preserve's entrance on the right.

 website: **www.conservationhamilton.ca**

10

As we begin to understand just how valuable wetlands are, we are doing a *little* better at protecting those that are left. Occasionally we even make efforts to return lost wetlands to a more natural state or to create them when the opportunity arises. Such is the case with the Fletcher Creek Ecological Preserve, where part of the preserve includes the rehabilitation of an abandoned quarry.

Located in Puslinch Township along the southern edge of Wellington County, the 168-hectare preserve contains many important ecosystems, including part of the 765-hectare Fletcher Creek Swamp Forest. This swamp forest contains a variety of habitats including deciduous, coniferous and mixed swamps, wet meadow, thickets, ponds, streams and upland areas. These areas provide habitat for many species including rare and vulnerable species such as the pickerel frog and the red-headed woodpecker.

The headwaters of Fletcher Creek, a cold water creek and the headwater tributary of the Spencer Creek system, begin in the Fletcher Creek Swamp Forest. Numerous springs are contained within the swamp.

Owned and managed by the Hamilton Conservation Authority, the Fletcher Creek Ecological Preserve has been designated as an Environmentally Sensitive Area, a Provincially Significant Wetland and a Regionally Significant Area of Natural and Scientific Interest. Besides the swamp forest, other ecosystems found in the preserve include old fields, mixed upland forest and a calcareous fen.

Limestone was historically mined in this area but the quarry was abandoned in the 1930s. In 1987, the Hamilton Conservation Authority acquired the land, and in 1991 it was declared an ecological preserve. During 2004 and 2005, the abandoned quarry was

- *The rehabilitated quarry is now a calcareous fen.*

rehabilitated and a rare form of wetland was created—the calcareous fen.

Fens differ from bogs in that fens receive water from the surrounding watershed in the form of streams, creeks and groundwater, while precipitation is the main source of water in bogs. Calcareous fens are wetland ecosystems that are fed by groundwater that contains considerable calcium and magnesium carbonate. Species diversity in these ecosystems is unusually high.

The abandoned quarry provided a good opportunity to create a wetland—and an ecosystem that is particularly rare. The rehabilitation was done in three phases and involved removing topsoil, lowering the quarry walls, stabilizing the site, replacing the topsoil, planting calcium-loving, native plants including trees and shrubs that are found in calcareous fens, building a boardwalk and constructing interpretive signs.

As long as humans need rock and gravel, there will be quarries. These mining areas have a significant impact on the environment, but the destruction can be minimized. Ensuring that quarries are not allowed in environmentally sensitive areas and that they are kept to a reasonable size is a start. When the life of a quarry is over, it is also important to follow, or at least consider, the example of what has occurred with the Fletcher Creek Ecological Preserve.

The preserve is an example of how an old quarry can be rehabilitated to create rare, vital habitat. Setting aside the protected land to be used by the public for recreation activities such as hiking, nature appreciation, snowshoeing and cross-country skiing is another constructive way to protect the natural world.

The Fletcher Creek Ecological Preserve contains an approximately 3-kilometre trail system in two loops that are configured like a figure eight. The trail system allows the hiker access to old fields, cedar forests, Fletcher Creek and the old quarry ponds where there are interpretive signs about the quarry's rehabilitation.

Early in the afternoon on a warm day in August, our family set out from the preserve's entrance on Concession 7 and started hiking the level gravel trail. We passed through an old field containing wildflowers and shrubs. Not long into the hike we came to Fletcher Creek, where we stopped to relax in the lovely setting that includes a nice forest of eastern white cedars. A bridge took us over the creek, and we soon came upon the old concrete foundations of buildings that were associated with the rock quarry.

Soon after passing the old foundations we came upon the rehabilitated quarry itself, which is a few hectares in size. There are some good vantage points to look out over the site. The trails and boardwalks allow you to visit this interesting place, where springs keep some areas from freezing over. Surrounding the quarry's shallow waters are beautiful wetlands containing native wetland plants.

10

Hilton Falls Conservation Area

*Since the land is the parent, let the citizens take care of her
more carefully than children do their mother.*

—Plato

AT A GLANCE

- The extensive forest contained in this natural environment park is one of the largest in southern Ontario and features numerous different forest habitat types. Wetland communities, including wooded swamps, beaver ponds, streams and vernal pools also exist.

- Hilton Falls is a 10-metre high waterfall.

- The stone ruins of three 19th-century mills can be seen near the falls.

- Approximately 700 species of plants have been found in and around this conservation area.

Directions: From Highway 401, go north on Highway 25 to 5 Side Road (Campbellville Road) and proceed west on 5 Side Road (Campbellville Road) to the park's entrance.

 website: **www.conservationhalton.ca**

11

Established in 1971 and almost 650 hectares in size, Hilton Falls Conservation Area is located on the Niagara Escarpment in Milton. The extensive forest contained in this natural environment park is one of the largest in southern Ontario and features many different forest habitat types. Wetland communities, including wooded swamps, beaver ponds, streams and vernal pools (temporary wetlands created from melting snow and spring rains that provide breeding areas for frogs, salamanders and other animals) also exist. This large natural area also protects the headwaters of Sixteen Mile Creek.

The numerous types of habitat found within the park result in a rich diversity of species. Approximately 700 species of plants have been found in and around this conservation area, including the yellow lady's slipper.

Birds are also well represented, with more than 150 species having been recorded here including more than 20 species of warblers. Thirty species of mammals have been observed in this conservation area and its environs, including the northern flying squirrel, as well as 10 species of reptiles and 17 species of amphibians. A population of redside dace, also lives here. This fish is a species at risk. Hilton Falls is also one of the largest breeding sites in the province of the West Virginia white butterfly.

Of the impressive list of species found at Hilton Falls Conservation Area and its surrounding immediate area, more than 80 species of plants and animals are considered rare and more than 175 species are uncommon.

The conservation area, owned and managed by Conservation Halton, has been designated as a Life Science Area of Natural and Scientific Interest (ANSI), an Environmentally Sensitive Area and a Provincially Significant Wetland. This beautiful park is also important in that it provides a link to other natural areas in this region of rapid development.

● *A vernal pool in the park in spring*

One of this area's main attractions is the 10-metre-high waterfall. Flowing over the rock of the Niagara Escarpment is Sixteen Mile Creek. Hiking the Hilton Falls Trail takes you to the scenic waterfall where there are upper and lower viewing areas and interpretive signs to inform you about the site's history. A set of stairs takes you down to the creek and a good close-up view of the waterfall, the escarpment and the creek. The area by the falls is also a good place for a picnic or to rest and relax for a while.

The site around the falls has considerable history: three 19th-century mills were built here, and stone ruins still exist including part of a wall, called the Raceway Arch. The first mill was built by the conservation area's namesake—Edward Hilton. This early settler constructed a mill at the base of the falls in 1835. The mill supplied Nassagaweya Township with lumber but was abandoned and fell into disrepair. Hilton supported William Lyon Mackenzie in the Upper Canada Rebellion of 1837 and when the uprising failed, Hilton fled to the United States.

In 1856, this scenic property was acquired by Dr. George Park, who built another mill complete with a large waterwheel to power the mill. The operation was sold in 1857, and in 1860 the mill was lost to fire. The stone ruins still in existence are from this mill.

The third, and final, mill was constructed by John Richards. It began operation in 1863, but in 1867 it too was destroyed by fire.

Hilton Falls Conservation Area has more than 30 kilometres of trails that are part of a series of overlapping loops. Three of the trails are for hiking and cross-country skiing, and three are for cycling, so hikers

● *Hilton Falls with the mill ruins*

should stay off of them. The Bruce Trail also goes through the park.

The most popular hiking trail is the Hilton Falls Trail, which features old logging roads and paths that wind through scenic forests. It goes to Hilton Falls where there are benches, lookouts and interpretive signs. The Beaver Dam Trail is the longest trail in the park and it accesses wetlands and beaver meadows in the northern part of the conservation area. The trail also crosses

headwater areas of Sixteen Mile Creek. The Red Oak Trail is another hiking and cross-country ski trail that goes around Hilton Falls reservoir on old logging roads. The 14-hectare reservoir was constructed in 1971 for flood control.

Besides hiking and cycling, nature appreciation, photography and picnicking are popular activities in the park.

● Sixteen Mile Creek upstream from the falls in spring

Our family has been to Hilton Falls Conservation Area in January and April. On both occasions we found ourselves heading to Hilton Falls. At the end of January, we cross-country skied to the falls on the Hilton Falls Trail. The snow on the trail was well packed, which would have been good for hiking as well. Because the deciduous trees were bare, we could see well into the forests. When we reached Hilton Falls, we took our skis off and enjoyed the frozen falls from the viewing areas. The cedar trees growing on the rocks around the falls provided an attractive green background to the snowy environment. The creek downstream from the falls also made a picturesque scene. We returned to Hilton Falls in mid-April and the cool, sunny day made for a nice, brisk walk to the falls. The deciduous trees were still bare, but the snow had recently melted exposing moss-covered rocks and creating vernal pools in the woods. As a result of snowmelt and spring rains, there was an impressive volume of water flowing over the rock of Hilton Falls. We admired the waterfall and the creek above and below the falls for some time before returning to the parking lot.

11

When we left the parking lot, I couldn't help but notice that within a few minutes' drive of the conservation area we were in the middle of a busy, urban area and one that is growing rapidly. This conservative area, which links to other natural areas, plays a crucial role in protecting habitat, significant geologic formations and many plants and animals while providing us with a refuge for exercising and enjoying the wonders of the natural world.

● *Hilton Falls in winter*

Terra Cotta Conservation Area

*I would feel more optimistic about a bright future for man
if he spent less time proving that he can outwit Nature and more time
tasting her sweetness and respecting her seniority.*

—E.B. White

AT A GLANCE

- Terra Cotta Conservation Area features a good trail system containing seven trails, including a section of the Bruce Trail.

- The more than 200-hectare natural environment conservation area contains significant natural features and rugged topography including rivers, lakes and ponds.

- Terra Cotta's waterways include cold water and warm water fish habitat.

- The Wetland Trail takes you around the human-made, restored wetland ecosystem. This is a fun trail to introduce young children to wetland ecosystems and their importance.

Directions: Terra Cotta Conservation Area is located on Winston Churchill Blvd. north of Terra Cotta. From Highway 401 exit north on Winston Churchill Blvd. and veer slightly north on King Street and then turn west on Winston Churchill Blvd. and proceed to the park.

 website: **www.creditvalleyca.ca**

Recent decades have seen some parks and conservation areas revert to a more natural environment by removing human-made structures and allowing landscaped areas to return to nature. Such is the case with Terra Cotta Conservation Area.

Located just north of the village of Terra Cotta, the site was the home of the Terra Cotta Playground, which opened in 1949. This recreational facility was contained on a 40-hectare piece of land that featured a dance pavilion, an office, a concession building, rentable cabins, picnic tables and a 12-hectare pond. This commercial endeavour was created by Leo Wolf, and the largest of the conservation area's human-made ponds, Wolf Lake, bears his name.

Credit Valley Conservation purchased the property in 1958 and started to acquire land for what became Terra Cotta Conservation Area. They maintained the recreational philosophy of

● *A wetland replaced the swimming pool*

the property for the next few decades, and during the 1980s, the conservation area contained well over a hundred unserviced campsites, hundreds of picnic tables, a one-acre swimming pool, a visitor centre, a concession stand and mini-golf. The popular recreation spot had parking to accommodate 650 cars.

Fortunately for the ecosystems and habitats on the property, a new philosophy was taking over—one that placed an emphasis on protecting environmentally significant areas. By the mid-1990s, the camping facilities at Terra Cotta Conservation Area were gone and the land was allowed to return to a more natural state. The large swimming pool was also removed. In its place a wetland was created. This habitat restoration project earned Credit Valley Conservation a Niagara Escarpment Achievement Award. Working together with Credit Valley Conservation to keep the park natural and provide educational opportunities is the volunteer group Friends of Terra Cotta.

Terra Cotta's waterways include cold water and warm water fish habitat. Another important naturalization project of Credit Valley Conservation involves restoring the native brook trout in the cold water habitat by naturalizing, bypassing or removing human-made ponds in the conservation area to provide cold water downstream for the trout, who require clean cold water streams.

Today the more than 200-hectare natural environment conservation area contains significant natural features and rugged topography including rivers, lakes and ponds as well as Provincially

12

Significant Areas of Natural and Scientific Interest (ANSIs).

As well as its numerous waterways, Terra Cotta Conservation Area has a good trail system with seven trails, including a section of the Bruce Trail. Trail lengths vary from a little over 500 metres for the Wetland Trail to more than 3 kilometres for Terra Cotta Lane, an easy loop trail that goes along the shore of Wolf Lake, circling the lake and accessing other trails.

The Wetland Trail begins near the parking area and takes you around the human-made, restored wetland ecosystem where the large swimming pool once existed. This fun trail introduces young children to wetland ecosystems and their importance.

Other trails in the conservation area include the A.F. Coventry Nature Trail, which passes through forest communities; the Vaughn Trail, which accesses mature forest stands; the McGregor Spring Pond Trail, a loop around Spring Pond and Muskrat Pond that goes through mixed deciduous forest; and the Graydon Trail, which accesses valley edges, conifer plantations and mature forests. There is also approximately 1.5 kilometres of the Bruce Trail, which takes hikers to ponds and exposed red clay hills. In winter, some of the trails are designated for cross-country skiing.

Other activities in the park include photography, nature appreciation, picnicking, snowshoeing and skating, when the ice conditions permit it.

Lynn and I arrived at Terra Cotta Conservation Area early one afternoon at the end of August. We set out on the Wetland Trail, where from boardwalks we observed ponds covered with water lilies. This wetland, which is home to turtles, frogs and various other animals, was a fun and interesting place to visit.

Next, we hiked the entire east shore of Wolf Lake along Terra Cotta Lane—an easy stroll along an old road through forests and with nice views of Wolf Lake. We also visited Muskrat Pond, where we saw frogs and other animals.

We were impressed with the natural state of this conservation area. It is hard to imagine that a large swimming pool, parking for 650 vehicles and various other commercial amenities existed here in recent decades. Although we enjoyed our time in the park, we barely touched the approximately 12 kilometres of trails and would like to return to walk these paths.

● *American bullfrog*

Elora Gorge Conservation Area

A river is more than an amenity, it is a treasure.

—Oliver Wendell Holmes

AT A GLANCE

- The 200-hectare Elora Gorge Conservation Area offers lots of activities including hiking and camping, but the most popular and fun way to enjoy the scenery is to float down the Grand River inside the park on an inner tube.

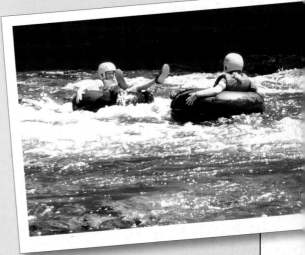

- The Grand River watershed is the largest watershed in southern Ontario.

- The park opened in July 1954 and was the first park of The Grand Valley Conservation Authority, which is now the Grand River Conservation Authority.

Directions: Take Wellington County Road 7 into Elora and turn west onto Wellington County Road 21. The conservation area is located at 7400 Wellington County Road 21.

website: **www.grandriver.ca**

Located southwest of the village of Elora and governed by the Grand River Conservation Authority, the 200-hectare Elora Gorge Conservation Area offers many activities including hiking, camping and tubing. Flowing through the 22-metre-high cliffs of the Elora Gorge is the Grand River.

This area was an inland sea some 410 million years ago. Coral reefs grew and were home to molluscs, and these molluscs and coral reefs have formed some of the limestone cliffs of the Elora Gorge. Fast forward to only tens of thousands of years ago when the climate cooled considerably and a glacier more than a kilometre thick lay over the gorge. When the glacier began to melt and retreat, approximately 16,000 years ago, the meltwater carved a path through the limestone. The glacier had disappeared by about 10,000 years ago, leaving the spectacular rock formations of the Elora Gorge.

The Elora Gorge Park opened in July 1954 and was the first park of The Grand Valley Conservation Authority, now the Grand River Conservation Authority. Ideas for creating a public park at the gorge were initiated as early as the 1870s and then again in the 1930s and 1940s. A 121-hectare strip of land along the river was purchased in 1953, and additional land was purchased in the 1980s to provide more space for camping.

Although the limestone cliffs are a popular feature of the park, so too is the Grand River. At almost 7000 square kilometres, the Grand River watershed is the largest in southern Ontario. Major rivers that are a part of this watershed include the Conestogo, the Eramosa, the Speed and the Nith rivers.

The Grand River watershed begins near the town of Dundalk in the north, includes the large Luther Marsh, and flows south close to 300 kilometres to Port Maitland on Lake Erie. It is home to numerous species at risk, has more than 80 species of fish and is a Canadian Heritage River.

A popular and fun way to enjoy the scenery of the park is to float down the Grand River inside the park on

● *The Grand River through Elora Gorge*

an inner tube. The approximately 2-kilometre section of the river where tubing occurs contains some rapids and turbulent areas as well as some calm areas and provides a refreshing way to experience the park. When tubing in the Elora Gorge Conservation Area, you can't help but be in awe of how water has sculpted this gorge.

You can rent equipment at the park on a first-come first-served basis. As well as an inner tube you must have a helmet and a life jacket, and secure footwear is recommended. Participants must pre-register for tubing and sign a waiver. There is also a minimum height requirement.

Tubing is only permitted when river conditions are safe for this activity, so it is not always available. There are also risks to tubing. Besides the turbulent areas, there are rocks below the water surface and other hazards. Every-

one tubing on the Grand River must have adequate swimming skills and be in good physical condition. Not only are there no lifeguards or river patrol staff, but there are also no entry or exit points along the tubing course because of the deep gorge. Once you begin the course, you are committed to finishing it. Current tubing information can be obtained by contacting the Elora Gorge Conservation Area.

13

Other popular activities besides tubing are camping, picnics and hiking. Several short trails provide access to lookouts with stunning views of the Grand River. Because of the potential dangers, you must stay on the trails, away from the gorge and behind the safety barriers. The Hole in the Rock, a natural passageway through limestone cliffs, is definitely worth seeing.

● *Hole in the Rock*

Our family eagerly awaited our visit to the Elora Gorge Conservation Area. I was looking forward to seeing, and photographing, the Elora Gorge and the Grand River. Lynn, Gleannan and Liam were also excited about visiting this park, but they were particularly looking forward to tubing down the Grand River. On this warm August day, I was designated photographer and would enjoy the river from its scenic shores.

After acquiring their inner tubes, helmets and life jackets from the conservation area and signing waivers, Lynn, Gleannan and Liam launched their tubes at the start of the course where there are some rapids. Gleannan successfully made her way through the rapids. Liam was next and he got stuck in the turbulent waters and was accidently knocked off his inner tube when Lynn came through the rapids. After Liam climbed back on his inner tube, they continued on their river adventure.

The course features some calm waters as well as other turbulent sections to go along with the spectacular scenery. Lynn, Liam and Gleannan all agreed that tubing on the Grand River in the Elora Gorge Conservation Area was an exciting and fun experience.

After returning the tubing equipment, we hiked some of the short trails near the Hole in the Rock. The trails were easy and provided great views of the Elora

13

- *Tubing downriver*

Gorge and the Grand River below. The Hole in the Rock, and the area around it, was fun to explore. Stairs through the rock take you to an area where you can enjoy the limestone cliffs. There are numerous eastern white cedars clinging to the rocks here as their extensive and remarkable root systems grow over the rock in search of soil.

13

● *Eastern white cedars growing on rocks*

The Elora Cataract Trailway

On Spaceship Earth there are no passengers;
everybody is a member of the crew. We have moved into an age
in which everybody's activities affect everybody else.

—Marshall McLuhan

AT A GLANCE

- The Elora Cataract Trailway is a linear 47-kilometre-long greenbelt that extends from Elora to Cataract.

- The 3-metre-wide, multi-use trail goes through forests, wetlands, meadows, ponds and lakes as well as eight municipalities in three counties.

- The entire trail is open to hikers, cyclists, wheelchairs, skiers and snowshoers, and some sections are also open to equestrians at specified times of the year.

- The Shand Dam was the first multipurpose dam in Canada.

Directions: There are many access points for this trailway including parking lots in Elora, Fergus, Belwood, Orton, Hillsburgh, Erin and Cataract.

website: **Elora Cataract Trailway Association**
www.trailway.org

Grand River Conservation Authority
www.grandriver.ca

Credit Valley Conservation
www.creditvalleyca.ca

Created from an abandoned Canadian Pacific Railway bed, the Elora Cataract Trailway is a linear trail, 47-kilometres long, that is owned by the Grand River Conservation Authority and Credit Valley Conservation. These conservation authorities, which acquired the abandoned railway lines in 1993, manage the trail along with the Elora Cataract Trailway Association.

This linear greenbelt extends from the town of Elora to the village of Cataract and provides a scenic trail for people to enjoy and a nature corridor for other species to travel through. The trail passes through Hillsburgh, Orton, Belwood and Fergus as well as three parks—Elora Gorge Conservation Area, Belwood Lake Conservation Area and Forks of the Credit Provincial Park.

Besides linking several communities, the 3-metre-wide, multi-use greenway goes through forests, wetlands, meadows, ponds and lakes as well as eight municipalities in three counties. The trailway also links the Grand River and Credit River watersheds. The entire trail is open to hikers, cyclists, skiers, snowshoers and people in wheelchairs, and some sections are also open to equestrians at specified times of the year. The trailway can be accessed in numerous areas including parking lots in Elora, Fergus, Belwood, Orton, Hillsburgh, Erin and Cataract.

The trail begins in Elora with a parking lot and a kiosk at Gerrie Road. Heading east, the trail goes into Fergus, where signs indicate where you go on the streets. East of Fergus, the stone dust trail continues going to the Shand Dam in the Belwood Lake Conservation Area.

The Shand Dam was the first multipurpose dam in Canada. Completed in 1942 and operated by the Grand River Conservation Authority, the dam was constructed for both flood protection and a supply of water.

Belwood Lake Conservation Area is more than 200 hectares in size and features Lake Belwood, a 12-kilometre-long reservoir. Hiking, boating, swimming and picnicking are popular activities in the conservation area.

Heading southeast from the village of Belwood, the Elora Cataract Trailway passes through Orton, Hillsburgh and

14

- *Shand Dam*

Erin before heading northeast to Cataract. If you continue on, you will enter the Forks of the Credit Provincial Park, where you can see the Cataract Falls and access the Bruce Trail.

We've enjoyed hiking several sections of the wide, largely flat trail. In November, my two brothers, my cousin and I hiked the trail near Belwood. It was a nice, sunny day and the walk near Lake Belwood was a scenic one. In early spring, Lynn and I hiked another section of the trail near the lake. The easy hike was an enjoyable way to spend part of a spring day.

Next, Lynn and I explored the Elora Cataract Trailway in the Belwood Lake Conservation Area. The section of trail near the Shand Dam was particularly interesting. Not only was the lake quiet on the April afternoon, but the dam and the Grand River were also good places to visit. We descended the stairs, trying to avoid spray from the dam, down to the river. With the Grand River on one side of the dam and Lake Belwood on the other, this spot was a picturesque stop on the trailway.

Our next stop was the Elora section of the trail at the Gerrie Road parking lot. This location is the trailhead of the Elora Cataract Trailway. As with the other areas of the trailway that we visited, the path was wide, level and well maintained.

The trail near Cataract was our final **14** stop. We strolled through areas of cedar trees and next to wetlands until we got to where the Elora Cataract Trailway ends at the Forks of the Credit Provincial Park.

The modes of transportation allowed on the trailway have little impact on the environment. Although we have enjoyed hiking sections of this trailway, we plan on exploring it by bike in the future.

● *Belwood Lake near the village of Belwood*

Forks of the Credit Provincial Park

There is delight in the hardy life of the open.
There are no words that can tell the hidden spirit of the wilderness,
that can reveal its mystery, its melancholy and its charm.

—Theodore Roosevelt

AT A GLANCE

- Forks of the Credit Provincial Park is a 282-hectare, natural environment park containing numerous natural, cultural and recreational features including trails, various habitats, a waterfall, a kettle lake, a river, the ruins of a powerhouse, mill and dam, and the Credit Valley Railroad.

- Also known as Churches Falls, Cataract Falls is a scenic waterfall that has water from the Credit River spilling over the Niagara Escarpment.

- The park is home to numerous plant and animal species including rare species of plants and trout populations in the Credit River.

Directions: Take Highway 10 to Caledon. Proceed west on Charleston Sideroad (Regional Road 24). Turn south on McLaren Road and follow the signs to the park.

website: **www.ontarioparks.com/english/fork.html**

Where two branches of the Credit River come together near Cataract is Forks of the Credit Provincial Park. This 282-hectare park has many natural, cultural and recreational features including numerous trails, various habitats, a waterfall, a river and the ruins of a powerhouse, mill and dam. Some of the habitats include meadow, kame hills, forests, a kettle lake, a fast-flowing river and wetlands. Part of the Caledon Meltwater Channel Complex, an Earth Science Area of Natural and Scientific Interest (ANSI) is also contained in the park.

The park is home to numerous plant and animal species including rare species of plants and trout populations in the Credit River.

Also known as Churches Falls, Cataract Falls is a scenic waterfall that has water from the Credit River spilling over the Niagara Escarpment. A trail takes you to a viewing area where you can see the falls.

Recreation opportunities within the day-use park include hiking, biking, picnicking, nature appreciation and photography. In winter, cross-country skiing and snowshoeing are the best ways to see the park. Six trails, including the Bruce Trail, run through many areas of the park. Interpretive signs and viewing platforms complement the trails.

Another historical feature in the park is the Credit Valley Railway (CVR). The CVR was completed in 1879 and was part of the Streetsville to Orangeville line. The line included a wooden trestle at the Credit Forks, which is where the West Credit and the Credit rivers meet

15

● *A bridge over Credit River*

at Dominion Road. During the late 1880s, sandstone and limestone from several area quarries was transported to Toronto for building projects.

Lynn and I first went to Forks of the Credit Provincial Park after hiking the eastern end of the Elora Cataract Trailway. We entered the west side of the park on the trail, which is a section of the Trans Canada Trail. It was early spring, so deciduous trees were still bare and we had good views into the forests and along the spectacular gorge. It wasn't easy to get a good view of Cataract Falls, but what view we did get was impressive.

It was late summer when Lynn, Liam, Gleannan and I explored Forks of the Credit Provincial Park near the park's entrance on McLaren Road. We started out on the Trans Canada Trail and then switched to the Meadow Trail. Views of the kettle lake were beautiful. Set in a meadow with plants, shrubs and small trees, the lake was created when the glaciers retreated some 12,000 years ago.

Kettle lakes formed when a large piece of ice from the glaciers was left behind. When the ice chunk, which was partially or entirely buried under gravel and sand, melted, the depression in the ground filled with water. Kettle lakes receive water from snowmelt and rainwater.

Taking the Kettle Trail off of the Meadow Trail provided us with nice views of the lake from an elevated spot in the meadow. Lots of plants and shrubs held

our interest and we passed by some remnants of a house. The area was surveyed in 1818, and this site was the home of a family of settlers. An interpretive sign informs the hiker that the family of six who settled near the lake took almost 40 years to clear 8 hectares of trees from around the house.

Hiking the Trans Canada Trail to the Meadow Trail and switching to the Kettle Trail before returning to the parking lot on the Trans Canada Trail was a nice loop that went around the kettle lake. Milkweed plants were plentiful, as were apple trees. We walked at a leisurely pace, took lots of photographs and stopped frequently to admire the views; the hike took us about 75 minutes to complete.

We enjoyed our visits to Forks of the Credit Provincial Park and plan on returning to hike more of the extensive trail system in the park.

● *Remnants of a settler's house*

15

Island Lake Conservation Area

Only by confronting the enormity and unsustainability of our impact on the biosphere will we take the search for alternative ways to live as seriously as we must.

—David Suzuki

AT A GLANCE

- The main feature of the 332-hectare Island Lake Conservation Area is Island Lake. This 182-hectare reservoir was created in 1967 when two dams were constructed at the west end of the lake.

- Canoeing and kayaking are popular activities in the conservation area, as are hiking, picnicking, cycling and bird watching.

- The conservation area contains bogs, marshes, rivers, creeks, mature forests and meadows.

Directions: Take Highway 10 into Orangeville and go east on Buena Vista Drive. Turn north on Hurontario Street and follow the signs to the park entrance.

 website: **www.creditvalleyca.ca**

16

Located in the towns of Orangeville and Mono is Island Lake Conservation Area. The main feature of the 332-hectare conservation area is Island Lake. This 182-hectare reservoir was created in 1967 when two dams were constructed at the west end of the lake. The dams were built to control water flow into the Credit River, and when they went into operation, they created the lake by flooding the area, which had consisted of a small lake, a large cedar swamp and a deciduous thicket. In 1970, Island Lake Conservation Area was opened to the public.

Besides the human-made lake, the conservation area contains other wetlands including bogs, marshes, rivers and creeks. These wetland ecosystems are part of the provincially significant Orangeville Wetland Complex.

The conservation area is not all water and wetlands, however. It also has mature forests and meadows. Trails go along the lake and through forests and other interesting places within the park.

The variety of habitats within Island Lake Conservation Area results in an impressive diversity of animals and plants. Some of the birds known to frequent this area include ospreys, wood ducks and great blue herons. Red foxes and raccoons have been recorded in the park, and painted turtles, snapping turtles, northern leopard frogs and many other animals make this Environmentally Sensitive Area home. Residing in the lake, along with a variety of aquatic plants, are such fish as northern pike and yellow perch. Plants in the park include numerous species of trees, wildflowers and even carnivorous plants such as the pitcher plant and the sundew plant that live in bogs.

Canoeing and kayaking are popular activities in the conservation area, as are hiking, picnicking, cycling and bird watching. In winter, cross-country skiing, snowshoeing and skating are ways to enjoy this park. In an area that is rapidly losing rural landscapes to subdivisions and other developments, Island Lake Conservation Area provides people of all ages with a place to enjoy nature.

Many of the trees in the park had begun to turn colour when Lynn and I went for a canoe trip around Island Lake in mid-October. The conservation area was one of the busier areas that we've visited, with many people renting canoes on the sunny autumn day.

As we set off from the boat launch area, the atmosphere wasn't that of a tranquil lake; many other people in boats were in this busy part of the reservoir. The farther we got from the dock area, as we paddled in a northeast direction, the fewer boats we saw. After passing by several scenic islands, we had left most of the boats behind, and we started to relax on the calm lake.

raccoon

Canada Geese taking off and landing on the lake were fascinating to watch. The islands and some of the shoreline reminded me of lakes farther north as the images of the colourful trees reflected off the smooth surface of the water. Complementing the colours of the deciduous trees were the deep greens of the coniferous trees. We thoroughly enjoyed slowly paddling around the lake.

After our canoe trip, we hiked some of the Sugar Bush Trail. This scenic trail goes through a mature beech-maple forest where syrup is still gathered from the maple trees. The trees were striking on this fall day, and we enjoyed walking the leaf-covered trail. We also hiked some of the Memorial Forest Trail before leaving for home.

● *Sugar Bush Trail*

16

Hockley Valley Provincial Nature Reserve

In the woods a man casts off his years, as a snake his slough,
and at what period soever of life, is always a child.

—Ralph Waldo Emerson

AT A GLANCE

- The Hockley Valley Provincial Nature Reserve is composed of 378 hectares of spectacular forests, valleys, ridges, streams, rivers, swamps and meadows.

- The reserve is also home to a great diversity of animals including the locally-rare northern long-eared bat, the northern brook lamprey and the Jefferson salamander.

- More than 400 species of vascular plants can be found within the reserve.

17

Directions: The parking lot of the Hockley Valley Provincial Nature Reserve is located on the north side of Hockley Road, just east of the 2nd Line, between Airport Road and Highway 10.

 website: **www.ontarioparks.com/english/hock.html**

● *A trail in summer*

A wonderful place to go for a hike and appreciate nature is the Hockley Valley Provincial Nature Reserve. Established in 1989 and located northeast of Orangeville, this reserve is composed of 378 hectares of spectacular forests, valleys, ridges, streams, rivers, swamps and meadows. The reserve is an important part of the Niagara Escarpment Parks and Open Space System (NEPOSS). NEPOSS protects natural and cultural sites along the Niagara Escarpment.

There are four trails within the nature reserve: the main Bruce Trail corridor is approximately 5 kilometres long, and three side trails—the Tom East Side Trail, the Glen Cross Side Trail and the Snell Loop—provide approximately 7 more kilometres of trails. These footpaths allow you to visit the many diverse and important ecosystems. The rolling woodlands offer wonderful views, particularly from the ridges, while providing hikers with a good cardio workout. The streams and branches of the Nottawasaga River are beautiful and offer nice spots to take a break and enjoy the natural surroundings. If you don't want to hike all of the trails at once—which would be a significant effort—the Tom East Side Trail provides a scenic stroll in the woods.

Although the reserve is popular in autumn when the hardwood forests put on a display of brilliant colour, it is worth visiting this scenic park during other times of the year as well.

Hockley Valley is important for many reasons. It is classified as a nature reserve class park because it is a good example of distinct natural habitat and landforms along the Niagara Escarpment. Not only is this protected area aesthetically pleasing, it is also used for educational purposes, and it protects the gene pools of the species that live here—and there are many.

More than 400 species of vascular plants can be found within the reserve, including rare species such as the cuckoo flower and the hooked violet. Some of the trees in the reserve include stands of white cedar, sugar maple forests, white ash, beech, birch, hemlock, basswood, butternut, black cherry, balsam fir and trembling aspen. The reserve is also home to a great diversity of animals including the locally rare northern long-eared bat, the northern brook lamprey and the Jefferson salamander.

A nice feature of the reserve is that it is kept in a mostly natural state. Dead trees are left standing and provide homes, shelter and food for animals. Fallen trees are also left in place for mosses, fungi, insects and other animals who require decaying wood.

17

Protecting the reserve's ecosystems from human activity is another important aspect of this park. Camping, mountain biking, hunting, snowmobiling and all-terrain and off-road vehicles are prohibited. Hiking, nature appreciation, snowshoeing and cross-country skiing are permitted activities.

Thanks to the good trails, diverse ecosystems and natural state of this reserve, visitors can't help but get a greater appreciation and respect for the natural world while enjoying a fun day in a special place.

Lynn, Gleannan, Liam and I first visited this reserve in summer. After parking the car in the parking lot located approximately 250 metres east of the reserve, we entered the reserve by taking the Bruce Trail to the Tom East Side Trail. The Tom East Side Trail rejoins the Bruce Trail, creating a nice loop. Walking through mature rolling hardwood forests as well as meadows full of wildflowers and other plants was an enjoyable way to spend an afternoon. The dense canopy created by mature maple, beech and ash trees provided good protection from the sun. We enjoyed our hike so much that we returned a few days later for another walk.

Late autumn is also a good time to visit the reserve. My two brothers, my cousin and I explored the park on a sunny day in November. The day was crisp and clear, and the trails looked much different than what I had seen in the summer. The lush green environment had been replaced with hills covered in fallen leaves. Giant, bare trees cast long shadows. But not all of the plants had packed it in for winter. Green ferns and mosses stood out in contrast to the bed of brown leaves that covered the forest floor. During this hike we also walked the Tom East Side Trail, but we ventured farther on part of the Glen Cross Side Trail. This scenic trail crossed branches of the Nottawasaga River.

● *A branch of the Nottawasaga River*

17

Mono Cliffs Provincial Park

We must go out and re-ally ourselves to Nature every day.
We must take root, send out some little fibre at least,
even every winter day.

—Henry David Thoreau

AT A GLANCE

- The Niagara Escarpment makes a spectacular appearance in Mono Cliffs Provincial Park, where cliffs rise up 30 metres or more above the valley floor.

- Interesting geological features within the park include two bedrock outliers, a glacial spillway, ponds, streams and McCarston's Lake— a kettle lake.

- Designated as a Natural Environmental Park because of the recreational and educational experiences that it offers, Mono Cliffs Provincial Park is a trail-oriented park.

18

Directions: Take Airport Road to Dufferin County Road 8 and then go west to the 3rd Line E.H.S. and proceed north to the Mono Cliffs Provincial Park parking lot.

 website: **www.ontarioparks.com/english/mono.html**

Located northeast of Orangeville is Mono Cliffs Provincial Park. The 750-hectare park was created in the 1970s to preserve some of our biologically and geologically significant features. This park is part of the Niagara Escarpment Parks and Open Space System (NEPOSS) which protects natural and cultural sites along the Niagara Escarpment. The rock of the scenic Niagara Escarpment was formed over 400 million years ago and extends the entire length of the park.

Although the Niagara Escarpment is largely buried beneath glacial deposits in this area, it makes a spectacular appearance in Mono Cliffs Provincial Park, where cliffs rise 30 metres or more above the valley floor. The exposed escarpment features crevice caves, talus slopes and rock fissures. Other geological features within the park include two bedrock outliers, a glacial spillway, ponds, streams and McCarston's Lake.

Designated as a natural environmental park because of the recreational and educational experiences that it offers, Mono Cliffs Provincial Park is a trail-oriented park. Approximately 6 kilometres of the Bruce Trail runs through the central part of the park. Joining the Bruce Trail to form an impressive trail system are eight other trails: Walter Tovel Trail, McCarston's Lake Trail, Carriage Trail, Spillway Trail, Cliff Top Trail, South Outlier Trail, Lookout Trail and Link Trail. From these trails, park visitors can access many of the park's significant and beautiful features.

Development within the park has been kept to a minimum and, besides interpretive signs and display panels, includes stairways and viewing platforms.

While the diverse and spectacular scenery in Mono Cliffs Provincial Park is itself worth a visit, there are many other things to see. Part of the park's trail system was created from carriage trails and old roads. Our history is also evident

● *McCarston's Lake*

18

• *Jacob's Ladder*

glacial meltwater. These waters also created a spillway.

Located on the northern part of the Cliff Top Trail close to where it meets the McCarston's Lake Trail is a spot known as Jacob's Ladder, which is accessed by some metal stairs and wooden boardwalks. At Jacob's Ladder you can see cliff faces containing fossils; some 400 million years ago this rock was the base of an inland sea. There is also a viewing platform near Jacob's Ladder.

On the Lookout Trail, you can climb to one of the highest points in the park and have a good view.

in the form of rock walls, lime kilns and the foundations of homes.

Mono Cliffs park also has two outliers. These two islands of rock were created when they became detached from the escarpment as a result of glacial ice eroding the bedrock. The rocks were further eroded by rushing waters from

McCarston's Lake is also worth visiting. This kettle lake was created approximately 14,000 years ago when a large piece of buried ice from a retreating glacier melted. McCarston's Lake is the only natural lake in Mono Township.

The biological features of Mono Cliffs Provincial Park are also impressive. Numerous vegetation communities exist

• *Trilliums*

18

within the park, including deciduous and mixed forests, a variety of wetlands, coldwater streams and old fields. Growing along, and on, the cliffs are old-growth, eastern white cedar forests. Although the stunted trees don't appear old, they are hundreds of years old. More than 450 species of vascular plants live in the park, including more than 40 species of ferns. Numerous species of mammals, birds, reptiles, amphibians, fish and other animals also call the park home. Remains of animals have been discovered in the park's fissure system including those of a pika, a small rabbit-like mammal who today lives in the Rocky Mountains but who hasn't lived on the escarpment since the early Holocene, about 12,000 years ago.

pika

To minimize environmental impacts in the park, permitted activities are low impact and include hiking, nature appreciation and horseback riding (on designated trails) as well as cross-country skiing and snowshoeing in winter. The park is kept in a primarily natural state. Because the park contains many rare species of plants and has numerous dangerous and environmentally sensitive areas, it is particularly important to stay on the trails.

Our family has enjoyed Mono Cliffs Provincial Park on numerous occasions. The first time we hiked the park was in summer. We spent several hours visiting a variety of habitats including deciduous and mixed forests along with wetlands, old orchards and fields, ponds, McCarston's Lake and the escarpment.

The diversity of habitat within the park is incredible—you walk through old fields and orchards one minute and relax next to a pond or observe a cliff face a little while later, then hike through mature maple forests and then marvel at ancient cedar trees clinging to a rock.

Visiting McCarston's Lake was particularly enjoyable. We knew that we were approaching the kettle lake before we

● *A trail in May*

18

● *McCarston's Lake*

actually saw it because we could feel the refreshing, cool breeze coming off the water. Although I haven't been to Walden's Pond, which Henry David Thoreau wrote about, I imagine it to be similar to McCarston's Lake: a scenic lake surrounded by beautiful forests.

After spending some time relaxing next to the lake we headed to Jacob's Ladder and the viewing platform, which are both located fairly close to McCarston's Lake. The viewing platform offers incredible views over the park, so you may want to take some photographs. The cliff faces at Jacob's Ladder are also fascinating.

Autumn in Mono Cliffs Provincial Park is stunning, particularly when the fall colours are at, or near, their peak. Maple, beech and many other species of deciduous trees dressed in their fall finest and set amid the escarpment is a sight to behold.

Winter in the park is also beautiful. We have snowshoed and hiked the Cliff Top Trail to the viewing platform and then to McCarston's Lake on the McCarston's Lake Trail, where we looked out over the snow-covered lake.

18

Whether you are looking for some exercise, an educational family eco-adventure or an inspirational nature walk, you will find it on the trails of Mono Cliffs Provincial Park.

Luther Marsh Wildlife Management Area

In all things of nature there is something of the marvellous.

—Aristotle

AT A GLANCE

- At close to 6000 hectares in size, the Luther Marsh Wildlife Management Area is a large wetland located in the headwaters of the Grand River.

- Approximately 1500 hectares consists of open marsh and is known as Luther Lake.

- More than 240 species of birds have been observed in the area.

Directions: Take County Road 25 in the northern portion of Dufferin County to County Road 15 and go west on County Road 15. Turn south on Sideroad 21-22 East Luther and proceed to the wildlife management area on the west side of the road.

19

 website: **www.grandriver.ca**

■ At close to 6000 hectares in size, the Luther Marsh Wildlife Management Area is a large wetland located at the headwaters of the Grand River, which straddles Wellington County and Dufferin County. Approximately 1500 hectares consists of open marsh and is known as Luther Lake. This shallow lake is a warm-water system that features lots of aquatic vegetation, high nutrient levels and four islands.

Managed by the Grand River Conservation Authority and the Ministry of Natural Resources, the area is composed of a diversity of habitats including Luther Lake, swamps, bogs, a fen, forests and meadows. The reservoir has depths of up to 5.2 metres, although the average water level is a little more than a metre deep.

More than 240 species of birds have been observed in the Luther Marsh Wildlife Management Area. This popular wetland for birds is important for breeding, nesting and migrating birds. Some of the bird species recorded in the marsh include the mallard, wood duck, hooded merganser, black tern, common loon, black-crowned nightheron and double-crested cormorant. There is a large colony of great blue herons, and the bogs in the Wylde Lake area have breeding populations of Lincoln's sparrow.

Also found in Luther Marsh are 10 species of amphibians, including the mink

flying
squirrel

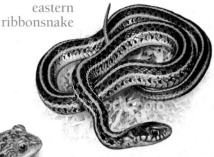

eastern
ribbonsnake

frog, 11 reptile species, 39 species of mammals and 18 species of fish. Four of the reptiles are provincially rare: the spotted turtle,

mink
frog

Blanding's turtle, Butler's gartersnake and the eastern ribbonsnake. Some of the mammals in the wildlife management area include the regionally rare bobcat and black bear as well as the northern flying squirrel. The fish species are mostly minnows, and there are also yellow perch and brown bullhead.

The Luther Marsh reservoir was built in 1952, mainly to increase low water flows in the Grand River but also to help with flood control. It took approximately two years to create Luther Lake over areas that previously included a cedar and tamarack swamp. Numerous stumps remain in the lake.

Bird watching is popular in Luther Marsh Wildlife Management Area because the area features many species along with large populations of birds that live, or stopover, here. Photography is another popular activity because the area offers photographers a good variety of animals and plants to photograph along with some stunning landscapes.

Hiking and cycling are two ways to see the marsh and its environs, and there are more than 20 kilometres of trail using the interior road network. Because of the numerous birds and other animals having and raising their young in this area, it is imperative that hikers and cyclists stay on the trail.

Luther Lake is a popular spot for canoes and kayaks, which are permitted on the lake after July 31. There are three canoe launches, but two are not accessible when the road is closed. Take care if you plan to canoe or kayak on the lake in fall because hunting is permitted in the wildlife management area. You should check with the Grand River Conservation Authority to learn which days are free of hunting, and go on these days to have a safe and more enjoyable experience.

Nature appreciation and picnicking are other activities to be enjoyed in the wildlife management area.

19

143

● *Exploring Luther Lake by canoe*

We have been to the Luther Marsh Wildlife Management Area on two occasions. Early in August, our family hiked some of the trail around the marsh. The shoreline vegetation was very tall at this time of year, so our best views over the lake were from the canoe launches and an observation tower.

In mid-September, Lynn and I decided to explore some of Luther Lake by canoe. Because it was a Sunday, there were no hunters at the marsh. In fact, only a few other people were in the area and they soon departed, leaving us with the scenic, shallow lake all to ourselves—and the hundreds of birds who were already there enjoying the warm, sunny day at the marsh.

When we set off from one of the canoe launches, evening was approaching. The scenery was stunning. The lake was relatively calm, and interesting clouds floated by. After paddling for a while we came across numerous gulls floating on the lake. A couple of birds appeared to be standing on the water, but as we got closer to the seemingly impressive feat, we realized they were standing on submerged logs that came up to the water's surface. We paddled along some of the marsh's shorelines and out into the open water. The atmosphere and views were spectacular as we slowly explored this interesting body of water.

19

We spent close to an hour and a half canoeing Luther Lake, and we covered only a small fraction of the open marsh. When we arrived back at the canoe launch, the sun was beginning to go down, providing a scenic, tranquil setting around the lake.

Lynn and I won't soon forget our enjoyable experience at Luther Lake, and we plan on returning to canoe the lake again. We also plan on hiking and biking the trails of this wildlife management area early in spring when views over the lake will not be impeded by the high, lush vegetation that surrounds the wetland in summer and fall.

● *Luther Lake on a September evening*

19

Nottawasaga Bluffs Conservation Area

Climb the mountains and get their good tidings.
Nature's peace will flow into you as the sunshine into the trees.
The winds will blow their freshness into you,
and the storms their energy, while cares will drop off like autumn leaves.

—John Muir

AT A GLANCE

- The Nottawasaga Bluffs Conservation Area is situated on the Niagara Escarpment and features swamps, old-growth cedars, deciduous forest and escarpment.

- Sections of a road created in 1846 still remain in the conservation area and are part of the trail system.

- This environmentally sensitive area is home to a large diversity of plant and animal species.

- This conservation area contains numerous areas that are very dangerous.

Directions: Take Highway 124 into Singhamton and turn east on Milltown Road and then east on Ewing Road. Turn east onto Nottawasaga 17/18 Sideroad, which curves south into Nottawasaga Concession 10 and then curves east into Nottawasaga 15/16 Sideroad. The parking lot is on the south side.

website: **www.nvca.on.ca**

www.nvca.on.ca/conservationareasrecreation

20

■ Located in Clearview Township near the village of Singhampton, the Nottawasaga Bluffs Conservation Area is about 161 hectares in size. Owned by Nottawasaga Valley Conservation Authority, this area is situated on the Niagara Escarpment and features swamps, old-growth cedars, deciduous forest and escarpment. The bluffs are some of the highest areas of the Niagara Escarpment; the main lookout is approximately 520 metres above sea level.

The conservation area and its environs contain natural areas that have been designated as Significant Wildlife Habitat and Life Science Area of Natural and Scientific Interest (ANSI) as well as being part of the Niagara Escarpment Biosphere Reserve.

Located within the conservation area is the Glen Huron Swamp, which features open-water beaver ponds and a conifer swamp of eastern white cedar and tamarack. Escarpment features include cliffs, crevices and slope forests.

Sections of a road created in 1846 still remain in the Nottawasaga Bluffs Conservation Area and are part of the trail system. Trails within the conservation area include the Ian Lang Trail and the Bruce Trail. There are approximately 5 kilometres of the main Bruce Trail and 2 more kilometres of Bruce Trail side trails in the conservation area.

Leys Burns Creek flows through the conservation area and is home to the brook trout. This creek is a tributary of the Mad River, which flows into the Nottawasaga River.

The Nottawasaga Bluffs Conservation Area is an environmentally sensitive area that is home to a large diversity of plant and animal species, including some rare and endangered species, such as tall goldenrod and heath aster. For this reason, only low-impact forms of recreation—hiking, nature appreciation, photography, bird watching, snowshoeing and cross-country skiing—are allowed.

The scenery in this conservation area is beautiful, but many areas are very dangerous. Rocks and roots on some sections of the trails might cause tripping, and although the lookouts provide good views, they are on cliffs with frightening drops. Make sure you stay on the trails, and if you take children ensure that they know of the dangers and are kept safe. Dogs must be kept on a leash for their safety and that of the animals who live in the area.

It is particularly important when visiting the conservation area in winter to stay on the trails and avoid rocky areas because crevices and chasms may be covered with snow.

We have visited this conservation area on several occasions. The first part of the trail is an easy walk through old fields. These meadows are slowly being reclaimed by various species of shrubs and trees including white pine and are full of wildflowers, raspberry bushes, apple trees and other plants.

It wasn't long before we came to the Keyhole Side Trail, which took us into a rocky area where high rock walls covered in mosses and ferns form narrow chasms or "canyons." The temperature in these areas is considerably colder, and during a hike in June we found some snow lingering in one of the canyons. Besides mosses and ferns, trees including old eastern white cedars cling to the rocks. Walking among these rocks and plants was both interesting and a lot of fun. You will want to take your time exploring this area, but be careful because the trail here is more difficult and it is slippery when wet. Liam sometimes gets bored on hikes, but not here. He enjoys exploring the canyons and scrambling over rocky areas while Gleannan is constantly taking photographs of the flora, fauna and geological features.

After leaving the canyons, we hiked the Nottawasaga Bluffs Side Trail to the main Bruce Trail, which goes out to the bluffs. Lookouts provide spectacular views, which will be even more impressive in autumn when the deciduous trees turn a wide array of colours to go along with the beautiful greens of the coniferous trees.

Lynn's parents, Audrey and Bob, accompanied us on a recent visit to the Nottawasaga Bluffs Conservation Area, and they also enjoyed the scenic hikes. Near the lookouts are caves and crevices, and it is amazing to see trees not only survive in these rocky areas with little soil, but thrive here.

● *Caves by the bluffs*

20

The Minesing Wetlands

Living is moving, time is a live creek bearing changing lights.

—Annie Dillard

AT A GLANCE

- The Minesing Wetlands are composed of swamps, fens, marshes as well as boreal and Carolinian forests.

- Canoeing is the main recreational activity within the wetlands.

- The wetlands are also home to more than 35 species of fish, eight species of reptiles, including six species of turtles, and close to 50 species of dragonflies and damselflies, as well as more than 40 species of butterflies.

Directions: There are various locations to access the Minesing Wetlands. The main canoe access point is Willow Creek, west of Barrie on George Johnston Road north of County Road 90. The parking lot is on the west side of the road. Canoe access is also available from the Edenvale Conservation Area on the north side of Highway 26 in the hamlet of Edenvale, located west of Barrie.

websites: **www.nvca.on.ca**
www.nvca.ca/conservationareascreation

21

Located west of Barrie is the 6000-hectare Minesing Wetlands. Wetlands are vital ecosystems, and these wetlands are one of the largest in southern Ontario, draining into Georgian Bay.

The significance of the Minesing Wetlands has not gone unnoticed. The result of post-glacial activity, these wetlands have been designated a Provincially Significant Wetland, a Life Science Area of Natural and Scientific Interest (ANSI) and Wetlands of International Importance.

As with other wetlands, the Minesing Wetlands have many important functions including their role in flood

● *Willow Creek*

protection, filtering out pollutants and maintaining water levels in area rivers and creeks. The Minesing Wetlands are composed of swamps, fens and marshes as well as boreal and Carolinian forests. The diversity of habitats within the wetland results in a high biodiversity that includes more than 520 plant species and more than 560 animal species. Many of these species are rare or endangered. Two plant species of concern are the eastern prairie white-fringed orchid and the butternut.

More than 30 species of mammals have been documented in the Minesing Wetlands, including the southern flying squirrel, fisher, Canada lynx, coyote, moose and black bear. These wetlands are also a large and important wintering ground for white-tailed deer.

Birds are also well represented in the Minesing Wetlands with more than 220 species having been documented here. These wetlands provide habitat for species at risk including the loggerhead shrike, olive-sided flycatcher, Cooper's hawk, Henslow's sparrow, short-eared owl, great gray owl, least bittern and several species of warblers. This area is also

an important staging area for migratory water birds and is home to one of the largest and oldest great blue heron colonies in Ontario.

Eight species of reptiles have been found in the Minesing Wetlands: the snapping turtle, midland painted turtle, northern map turtle, spotted turtle, wood turtle, Blanding's turtle, milk snake and eastern gartersnake. Many of the turtle species are species at risk.

Frogs make up the majority of the 10 amphibian species found in this ecosystem. The amphibians of these wetlands are the wood frog, northern leopard frog, mink frog, pickerel frog, green frog, western chorus frog, spring peeper, gray treefrog, American bullfrog and American toad. The western chorus frog is a species at risk.

As you would expect, there are many species of insects found in these wetlands. Of the more than 250 species, there are close to 50 species of dragonflies and damselflies as well as more than 40 species of butterflies.

The Minesing Wetlands are also home to more than 35 species of fish including non-natives such as common carp, coho salmon, rainbow trout and chinook salmon. Smallmouth bass, black crappie, northern pike and pumpkinseed are some of the native species that live in these wetlands. Species at risk found here include lake sturgeon and northern brook lamprey.

The Nottawasaga Valley Conservation Authority manages the wetlands.

great blue heron

21

Canoeing, hiking and nature appreciation are allowed in the area, and in winter cross-country skiing and snowshoeing are also permitted on some trails. Canoeing is the main recreational activity within the wetlands, and it is the most effective way to see much of this place. The main area to enter the wetlands by canoe is the Willow Creek access point on George Johnson Road north of County Road 90. Numerous other access points include Historic Fort Willow on Grenfel Road, off George Johnson Road, and the Edenvale Conservation Area on Highway 26. Historic Fort Willow is located on the Nine Mile Portage, a former transportation route between Lake Simcoe and Georgian Bay. This portage route passes through the Minesing Wetlands and was important to the British during the War of 1812.

Early spring is not a good time to canoe these wetlands unless you are experienced with a canoe and know the area very well. Even then you have to be wary—the area is flooded, making it easy to get away from the rivers and creeks and to get lost in this vast wilderness area. May usually results in the waters receding enough so that travel by canoe along the waterways in the wetlands is easier. If you plan on canoeing these wetlands in spring, you should contact the Nottawasaga Valley Conservation Authority to find out the water conditions.

Trails in and around the wetlands include the Meadow Mouse Interpretive Trail at the Willow Creek access point on George Johnson Road, the Ganaraska Trail, the Trans Canada Rail

● *Cows along the Nottawasaga River, outside the Minesing Wetlands*

Trail, the Portage Trail and the North Simcoe Rail Trail at Historic Fort Willow. There is also the McKinnon Trail, which is an unmaintained road allowance at the end of McKinnon Road off of County Road 90. The Mayer's Marsh Trail is on Vespra Valley Road.

Lynn and I set out from the Edenvale Conservation Area on a cool mid-September afternoon. The Nottawasaga River was calm, but it quickly became obvious that we were paddling against a fairly strong current as we headed south. After paddling under Highway 26, we left civilization behind.

The trees on the banks combined with the calm waters made for some lovely reflections on the river as we slowly made our way upstream towards the Minesing Wetlands. Although we hadn't yet entered the Minesing Wetlands, we were in an area with a rich biodiversity, so it seemed strange that some of the first animals we encountered were cows lying beside the river. Although we humans are getting better at protecting wetlands, much still needs to be done, as was evidenced from the eroded banks caused by the animals coming to the river to get a drink. Their manure also damages this fragile ecosystem.

For much of our trip up the river into the Minesing Wetlands, we were accompanied by several belted kingfishers. These attractive birds stayed just ahead of us, as if leading us into the wetlands. Every so often they would dive into the river after a fish.

Along the way we encountered a dragonfly struggling in the river so we stopped and rescued him, placing

● *Male arrow clubtail dragonfly*

him gently in the canoe to dry off. The dragonfly was a male arrow clubtail with an appetite. While drying off, the hungry insect found a cocoon on the bottom of the canoe and satisfied his hunger. When the dragonfly had dried off, we steered the canoe to a sunny bank with bushes and left our passenger on some branches.

Travelling the Nottawasaga River and Willow Creek by canoe was a great way to spend an afternoon. We saw only a few other people on the waterways as we paddled for more than two hours, which took us well into the Minesing Wetlands. Most of the Nottawasaga River and Willow Creek were easy to navigate, though there were numerous fallen trees in the river. Some trees had been down for some time—they were in various states of decomposition and other plants were growing on them. Besides occasionally having to man-oeuvre around some tree trunks and branches, there were few other difficulties on the river or the creek.

A couple of hours after setting out from the Edenvale Conservation Area we arrived at the spot where Willow Creek meets the Nottawasaga River. Fallen trees blocked our passage up the Nottawasaga River without a portage, so we paddled up Willow Creek for a while. Willow Creek is narrower than the Nottawasaga River, and parts of it are darker because the forested areas block out much of the sunlight. Most of the trees were still lush green, though some had started to change into their autumn colours. Eventually we reached

- *Tree reflections in Willow Creek*

some open areas where the creek was quite weedy.

We stopped our trip into the wetlands just before reaching the blue heron colony. The trip back went much faster. It was surprising the difference that the seemingly slow current made.

Our trip into the Minesing Wetlands was very enjoyable. We heard few sounds associated with civilization, and the atmosphere in this mostly undisturbed wilderness area was incredible. We felt great paddling the historic waterway. Getting out into this natural area was good for our psyche. When we initially arrived at the Edenvale Conservation Area, Lynn and I were both tired and stressed, but these feelings quickly evaporated as we started out on our wilderness adventure. Arriving back at the Edenvale Conservation Area we were a little tired, but we were also invigorated and excited about the nature outing that we just had. We plan to return soon.

● *Milkweed*

● *Willow Creek*

Grey County's Waterfall Tour

A river seems a magic thing.
A magic, moving, living part of the very earth itself.

22

—Laura Gilpin

AT A GLANCE

- The Grey County Waterfall Tour consists of a pleasant drive through the scenic countryside of Grey County where you can visit eight waterfalls.

- The waterfalls are Indian Falls, Jones Falls, Inglis Falls, Walters Falls, Eugenia Falls, Hoggs Falls, McGowan Falls and Weavers Creek Falls.

- The picturesque tour includes some potentially dangerous areas, particularly around the waterfalls.

- Visiting all eight waterfalls in one outing will take you the better part of a day.

Directions: See Below

 website: **www.visitgrey.ca/waterfalls**

If you are looking for something a little different for a nature outing, you might consider Grey County's waterfall tour. This tour allows you to drive through the scenic countryside of Grey County as you explore eight of nature's spectacular works of art where water flows over the Niagara Escarpment.

At each stop in the tour you can stretch your legs as you hike to the waterfall. Many of the waterfalls are close to the parking lot and involve about a one-minute walk to a viewing area. Others require a short hike varying from 5 to 15 minutes.

Waterfalls are fascinating places. It doesn't matter the size or shape of the waterfall, when a river or stream tumbles over a piece of exposed bedrock, the sights and sounds are breathtaking.

There are numerous types of waterfalls, including plunge, slide, cascade and ramp waterfalls. The waterfalls on this tour are one of two types—plunge or cascade. In a plunge waterfall, the water falls without contacting any rocks until it reaches the base of the waterfall. Cascade waterfalls occur when water flows over rocks in steps on the way down. These waterfalls are common in Ontario.

The eight waterfalls on the tour—Indian, Jones, Inglis, Walters, Eugenia, Hoggs, McGowan and Weavers Creek falls—consist of five plunge waterfalls and four cascade falls. If you are thinking that my math doesn't add up (and it often doesn't) it is because Weavers Creek Falls are both plunge and cascade. If you plan to visit all eight waterfalls in one outing, it will take you the better part of a day—especially if you like to explore a little and take some photos. The tour will take longer if you visit some of the towns, villages, stores and other attractions along the way. And if you want to photograph the falls when large amounts of water are spilling over the rocks, spring and autumn are good times to take the tour.

This tour has some potentially dangerous areas, particularly around the waterfalls, so be careful—especially if you take children.

Hoggs Falls

Directions: Take Highway 10 into Flesherton and turn east onto Grey Road 4 and then turn north onto East Back Line North. Go approximately one kilometre and turn east onto Lower Valley Road, then proceed for just under a kilometre to the parking lot.

Although it is only 7 metres high, Hoggs Falls on the Boyne River is my favourite waterfall on the tour. Set amid cedars, ferns and other plants, much of the attraction of this plunge waterfall lies in its natural, undeveloped setting, even though it is less than a five-minute walk from the parking lot. The scenic

22

location also features the ruins of an old mill. The falls are named after William Hogg who settled in this area in the 1870s. He was the son of the Hogg family of York, after whom Toronto's Hoggs Hollow is named.

Eugenia Falls

Directions: Take Grey Road 13 into the village of Eugenia, then turn left on Pellisier Street and follow the signs.

Just north of Hoggs Falls is Eugenia Falls. This spectacular plunge waterfall features water from the Beaver River falling approximately 30 metres into the Cuckoo Valley gorge. Discovered in 1852, this site had five mills and the province's second hydro-electric plant. The falls are named after Princess Eugenia, the wife of Napoleon III.

Located in the 23-hectare Eugenia Falls Conservation Area, the falls are complemented by walking trails and a picnic area. A picturesque stone wall keeps people back from the edge of the cliffs.

Walters Falls

Directions: Go into Walters Falls and turn north onto Front Street. Take the road into the parking lot next to the inn.

22

Discovered by John Walter in 1852, this double plunge waterfall is 14 metres high. Water from Walters Creek, a tributary of the Bighead River, drops into the gorge below.

Located next to an inn in the village of Walters Falls is a viewing platform above the falls that offers an interesting view. The commercial aspect made these falls the least appealing for me, but they're still worth a visit.

Inglis Falls

Directions: From the town of Rockford, go west on Grey Road 18, then turn north on Inglis Falls Road and follow the signs to the conservation area.

Named after Peter Inglis, who purchased the property in 1845, Inglis Falls is a beautiful cascade waterfall that has water from the Sydenham River spilling 18 metres over limestone rocks.

The Inglis family operated a sawmill, woollen mill and gristmill on this site from 1845 until 1934. The woollen mill was destroyed by fire around 1885, rebuilt and destroyed again by fire in 1901. The gristmill was destroyed by fire in 1945 but remnants of the building can still be seen. Located in the 200-hectare Inglis Falls Conservation Area, this site features walking trails, a picnic area and more than 20 species of ferns.

Weavers Creek Falls

22

Directions: In Owen Sound, take 2nd Avenue to Harrison Park. A trail and the boardwalk behind the pool lead you to the falls.

Plunge and cascade falls are both featured at Weavers Creek Falls in Owen Sound as water in Weavers Creek tumbles over rocks. The falls are accessed in Harrison Park, a 40-hectare park in Owen Sound that features trails, forest, streams, the Sydenham River, a bird sanctuary, a campground and much more. The park is named after John Harrison, who purchased the land in 1875, kept it in its natural state and opened it to the public.

It may take you some time to locate the falls, which are in an out-of-the-way part of the park. Look for the boardwalk that runs for approximately 300 metres behind the park's swimming pool. The boardwalk goes through a beautiful forested area where you can view the falls in a natural, relatively undisturbed setting.

Jones Falls

Directions: From Springmount turn right and go north on Highway 6 to the Visitor Information Centre, where there is parking.

Jones Falls is located in the 116-hectare Pottawatomi Conservation Area. The trail that leads to the falls is relatively short—approximately one kilometre long—and goes through old-growth forest. Of all the trails leading to waterfalls on this tour, this picturesque footpath is my favourite. The short hike

22

takes you to the cascade waterfall that sees the water from the Pottawatomi River flow down 12 metres of the Niagara Escarpment. Eastern white cedar, some hundreds of years old, along with boulders and rocky terrain help make this a special wilderness area in Grey County.

The falls are named after Samuel Jones, who constructed a sawmill on the river in 1849.

Indian Falls

Directions: From Owen Sound take Grey Road 1 north to the parking lot.

Next are Indian Falls. This spectacular waterfall is in the 12-hectare Indian Falls Conservation Area. A trail goes along the Indian River, where a set of stairs allows you to climb the gorge to get a good view of the falls. The rock formations of these falls are interesting because the soft, red Queenston shale has eroded below the harder Manitoulin dolomite cap rock.

22

McGowan Falls

Directions: In Durham, at the top of the hill, turn east onto Historic Durham Road (Grey Road 27) and drive to the conservation area.

McGowan Falls in the 60-hectare Durham Conservation Area is a 3-metre-high cascade waterfall on the Saugeen River. Hiking trails, a swimming area and picnic areas are provided.

Although the eight waterfalls on this tour can be seen in a day, especially if you get an early start, you may want to take your time and include other activities to go along with waterfall viewing. Hiking is popular, and most of the waterfall sites have good trails including the Bruce Trail. There is also no shortage of charming towns and villages to visit.

It was a pleasant May day when we began our waterfall tour. We got off to a slow start, leaving just before noon. Our plan was to begin at Hoggs Falls just east of Highway 10 near Flesherton and head north. Our second destination would be Eugenia Falls, located close to Hoggs Falls. Next would be Walters Falls, which is a little more out of the way, and then on to Inglis, Weavers Creek, Jones and Indian falls. These last four waterfalls are fairly close to one another in the Owen Sound area. The day we went, we had some difficulty getting to and from Indian falls. High water likely made part of the trail impassable, but some creativity on our part allowed us to see the scenic 15-metre waterfall where the Indian River plunges over the horseshoe-shaped waterfall. We observed these stunning falls, which are the most remote of the falls on the tour, for quite a while before returning to the parking lot—again with a little difficulty. We planned to finish our waterfall outing at McGowan Falls, the most southerly falls on the tour, located near Durham. Unfortunately, the tour took longer than expected, and McGowan Falls will have to wait for another day.

Meaford

In every walk with nature one receives far more than he seeks.

—John Muir

AT A GLANCE

- Beautiful Joe Park is a charming 3.4 hectare park on Edwin Street. The park was created in 1963 when the town of Meaford donated the scenic property along the Bighead River.

- The Trout Hollow Trail is an approximately 14-kilometre hiking trail that runs along both sides of the Bighead River. Steeped in history and very scenic, the trail follows the Bighead River Valley and contains sections that vary from easy to difficult.

- The Georgian Trail follows the shoreline of Georgian Bay and extends more than 32 kilometres from Collingwood to Meaford.

- The Tom Thomson Trail extends approximately 43 kilometres from Meaford to Owen Sound and is named after the famous painter who grew up in Leith near Owen Sound.

We first went to Meaford to visit Beautiful Joe Park, which pays tribute to the dog made famous in Margaret Marshall Saunders' literary classic *Beautiful Joe* as well as the author herself. While we were there we learned of the Trout Hollow Trail and returned several times to hike this scenic footpath with a fascinating history. Each time we visited this charming town and its environs, we found something else worth seeing, including the Georgian Trail, the Tom Thomson Trail and the waterfront.

23

Beautiful Joe Park

Directions: Beautiful Joe Park is located on Edwin Street. When driving west on Highway 26 (Sykes Street), turn left on Edwin Street and proceed to the parking lot.

website: **www.meaford.ca/beautiful-joe-home.html**

Margaret Marshall Saunders wrote *Beautiful Joe,* a classic children's story filled with humane messages, in 1893. It was the first Canadian book to sell a million copies. Beautiful Joe was a terrier-mix dog whose "master" cut off his ears and tail. Fortunately, the terribly abused dog was rescued and taken in by a kind family. Saunders learned about Joe while she was visiting her brother and his fiancée, Louise Moore, in Meaford. Moore's father, William, had rescued Joe from the cruel man who had mutilated the dog. William Moore owned the gristmill on the Bighead River close to where Beautiful Joe Park is situated. Joe was devoted to William Moore for the remaining 14 years that the mixed breed dog was alive.

When Saunders heard about a contest for a novel about animals sponsored by the American Humane Education Society, she wrote *Beautiful Joe* and won the $200 prize. Although the book is a novel, it is based on true events. The dog's actual name was Joe; Saunders added the "beautiful" to his name for her book. The story is set in Maine with the Morris family rescuing and caring for the abused dog, but the actual abuse and rescue occurred in Meaford. It is in this friendly, scenic town situated on Georgian Bay where Beautiful Joe Park exists.

Saunders was born in Milton, Nova Scotia, on May 13, 1861 and died on February 15, 1947 in Toronto. She was a supporter of women's and animals' rights and, together with Lucy Maud Montgomery, she co-founded the Maritime Branch of the Canadian Women's Press Club.

Saunders wrote more than 20 books and was awarded a Commander of the British Empire (CBE) in 1934. However, it is for her second book, *Beautiful Joe*, that Saunders is most remembered. This literary classic was chosen as one of the ten best children's books in Canada. *Beautiful Joe* has been translated into numerous languages.

Beautiful Joe Park is a charming 3.4-hectare park that was created in 1963 when the town of Meaford donated the scenic property along the Bighead River. Beautiful Joe's grave is in the park.

The Beautiful Joe Heritage Society was established in 1994 and one of the group's goals is to promote the humane treatment of animals.

23

Our family has visited this pleasant park next to the picturesque Bighead River with its mature trees and trails on several occasions. We have enjoyed visiting the statue of Beautiful Joe as well his cairn and some of the other memorials. It's a wonderful place that honours a faithful dog and the special bonds that exist between two species.

● *Bighead River bordering Beautiful Joe Park*

Trout Hollow Trail

Directions: There is a small parking lot across from Beautiful Joe Park where you can access the trail.

website: **www.bigheadriver.org**

23

The Trout Hollow Trail is an approximately 14-kilometre hiking trail that runs along both sides of the Bighead River. Steeped in history, the scenic trail follows the Bighead River Valley. The trail, named after the Trout family who once settled in the area, begins at the Bakeshop Bridge in Meaford (a small parking lot across from the entrance to Beautiful Joe Park) and follows the Bighead River to the Riverside Community Centre on the 7th Line of St. Vincent. Managed by the Bighead River Heritage Association, the trail goes through private property and

● *Bighead River along Trout Hollow Trail*

contains sections that vary from easy to difficult.

Located just off Edwin Street and north of the trailhead are some gristmill ruins from the Wm. Moore & Sons Flour Mill. It is the same William Moore who rescued Beautiful Joe. The mill was built in the 1840s and was demolished in 1933.

Other historical remains of structures on the trail include power house ruins and power dam ruins. The remains of the power dam are from a dam built in 1904 that provided electricity for Meaford. This dam was broken by a flood in 1912 and was rebuilt and continued working until 1923. The Flume Trail is a pleasant forested section of the Trout Hollow Trail that takes you to where ruins of the power house station still stand in the woods. This section of the trail is the route the water travelled from the power dam to the settling basin along a wooden flume. A piece of the massive pipe that carried water from the pond, created by the dam, to the power house still exists in the woods.

The Trout Hollow Trail also provides access to the site where the Trout Hollow sawmill, and later a gristmill, once stood. The sawmill was where famous American naturalist John Muir worked from 1864 to 1866 making rakes and broom handles. The Trout family took in John Muir and his brother Dan in 1864. Muir's ability to invent things included machinery that significantly increased production of the rakes and

23

● *Bighead River along Trout Hollow Trail, near power dam ruins*

broom handles. Unfortunately, the saw-mill was destroyed by fire in 1866 and Muir returned to the United States.

When he was not working in the saw-mill on the Bighead River, Muir was enjoying nature and studying plants. The time Muir spent in Canada was an important period in his life and helped to shape his philosophy regarding con-servation and the protection of the environment. When he returned to the United States, Muir's love of nature resulted in his making a huge contribu-tion to the natural world; he was largely responsible for the establishment of the national parks system in the United States. Muir was also a founder of the Sierra Club and served as its first president. He truly was a pioneer of the conservation movement.

● *Gleannan and Liam in a steel pipe near the power house ruins*

Our family has hiked the Trout Hollow Trail in summer and fall, and it is spec-tacular at these times with the sun dan-cing off the Bighead River along with the beauty of the fields and woodlands through which the trail goes. And you don't have to take my word for it. On May 23, 1865, John Muir wrote the fol-lowing to a friend while staying in Trout Hollow:

> *We live in a retired and roman-tic hollow...Our tall, tall forest trees are now all alive, and the ocean of mingled blossoms and leaves waves and curls and rises in rounded swells farther and farther away, like the thick smoke from a factory chimney. Freshness and beauty are every-where; flowers are born every hour; liv-ing sunlight is poured over all, and every thing and creature is glad. Our world is indeed a beautiful one...*

I like that much of the trail follows the Bighead River. I never tire of watch-ing this enchanting river, where each bend of the waterway holds another breathtaking scene. The winding river with fast and slow moving sections and lots of rocks is enjoyable to walk along. Knowing some of the history of the area adds to the walk.

We have hiked the trail near Beautiful Joe Park, where we walked through some woodlands and along the river. We have also accessed the trail at the 7th Line of St. Vincent and Sideroad 12/13, where there is parking for a few cars. This section of the trail passes through the ruins of the Trout family's sawmill in Trout Hollow.

● *A wall of the power house still stands in the woods.*

During an autumn hike along the section of the trail where John Muir lived and worked, we were given a tour of the area by Ron Knight, who owns the property. Ron showed us the ruins of the power dam and power house—both reminders of the Bighead River as a source of Meaford's electricity early in the 20th century. Ron also showed us where the Trout Hollow sawmill stood and the site of John Muir's cabin. Archaeologists have confirmed the location of Muir's cabin and the sawmill.

We also walked the Flume Trail section of the Trout Hollow Trail to where the power house existed. This pleasant fall afternoon hike not only provided us with good exercise in a scenic setting, but with a history lesson as well.

Georgian Trail

Directions: The Georgian Trail has many access points.

website: **www.georgiantrail.ca**

Following the shoreline of Georgian Bay, the Georgian Trail extends more than 32 kilometres from Collingwood to Meaford. The level trail runs parallel to Highway 26 and is built on an abandoned railway line. The trail passes through urban and rural settings including apple orchards, wetlands and forests. There are numerous access points, and the trailhead is at the Meaford Harbour. The trail is used for hiking, cycling, snowshoeing and cross-country skiing.

A particularly scenic location on the Georgian Trail is in Thornbury, where you have a wonderful view down the Beaver River to Georgian Bay from a bridge.

- *Georgian Trail*

Tom Thomson Trail

Directions: The Tom Thompson Trail has many access points.

 website: **www.tomthomsontrail.com**

The Tom Thomson Trail extends approximately 43 kilometres from Meaford to Owen Sound. Named after the famous painter who grew up in Leith near Owen Sound, this three-season (spring, summer and fall) trail is for hiking, cycling and horseback riding. The trailhead kiosk is in Fred Raper Park at the Meaford Harbour. Combined, the Tom Thomson Trail and the Georgian Trail provide a trail system that is approximately 75 kilometres long and extends from Collingwood to Owen Sound.

● *Hiking the Flume Trail*

Wye Marsh Wildlife Centre

Time in nature helps both the child and the parent by building their shared sense of attachment and by reducing stress.

—Richard Louv

AT A GLANCE

- The Wye Marsh Wildlife Centre is located on more than 1200 hectares of wetlands and forest on the edge of the Wye Valley.

- A success story at the centre involves efforts to restore trumpeter swans in the province.

- Numerous trails take you around the marsh and woodlands.

- Open all year, Wye Marsh also offers some winter adventures that allow visitors to experience the scenic marsh under snow and ice.

Directions: On Highway 400 north of Barrie take exit 121 (Highway 93). Go north on Highway 93 to Highway 12, and go east on Highway 12 into Midland past King and William streets then watch for signs. Wye Marsh is located across from Martyrs' Shrine.

 website: **www.wyemarsh.com**

Located on more than 1200 hectares of wetlands and forest on the edge of the Wye Valley is the Wye Marsh Wildlife Centre. Operated by the not-for-profit organization Friends of Wye Marsh, the environmental facility is dedicated to connecting people with nature and educating the public about the importance of wetlands.

Wye Marsh is part of the Wye River Watershed. The river passes through the Wye Valley and the Wye Marsh before entering Georgian Bay. This wetland is a fascinating and diverse ecosystem, and has been designated an Area of Natural and Scientific Interest (ANSI), an Important Bird Area (IBA), a National Wildlife Area and a Provincial Wildlife Area.

There is plenty to do at the Wye Marsh Wildlife Centre throughout the year. Hiking is a popular activity, and the nature walk not only provides good exercise but also lots of opportunities to view a wide array of animals and plants—and the views over the marsh are excellent. Numerous trails take you around the marsh and woodlands. The trails vary in length from just under 500 metres for the Arboretum Trail to almost 2 kilometres for the Boardwalk Trail and the Woodland Trail. The Ganaraska Trail also goes through the area. In all, the Wye Marsh has more than 20 kilometres of hiking and biking trails.

This special wetland can also be observed from the water in a guided canoe or kayak tour. For a longer paddle, visitors

24

- *The boardwalk into Wye Marsh in February*

can book an ecotour of Wye Marsh with one of the Wye Marsh guides. Ecotours are approximately three hours in length and take you well into the marsh.

Open year-round, Wye Marsh also offers some winter adventures, allowing visitors to experience the scenic marsh under snow and ice. There are numerous trails for snowshoeing and cross-country skiing. Longer outdoor adventures can include a snowshoe ecotour 3 to 4 kilometres into the woods at Wye Marsh. Bird watching, photography and nature appreciation are other low-impact activities that are popular at the marsh.

A success story at the Wye Marsh Wildlife Centre involves efforts to restore trumpeter swans in the province.

Although these magnificent birds once existed right across North America, their numbers were greatly reduced as a result of hunting and habitat loss. These large, mostly white birds with a black bill and black feet were extirpated from Ontario more than two centuries ago. In 1982, Harry Lumsden began a program to reintroduce trumpeter swans to Ontario, and in 1989 the Wye Marsh Wildlife Centre got involved with bringing this incredible bird back to Ontario. Archaeological evidence has proven that Trumpeter Swans lived in the Wye Valley.

Although reintroduction efforts have been successful, with more than a thousand of these striking birds now in Ontario, trumpeter swans are not

24

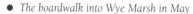

● *The boardwalk into Wye Marsh in May*

● *Trumpeter swans*

assured of a bright future. Wetlands continue to be lost, eliminating the swans' habitat. Also, hunting is permitted at Wye Marsh and wetlands across Canada. Although trumpeter swans are a protected species, many swans have suffered lead poisoning at Wye Marsh as a result of ingesting lead shot that was deposited here from past hunts, which they mistook for grit.

It was mid-May when our family first visited Wye Marsh. We were looking forward to exploring the area by hiking the trails, but our first adventure was a canoe ecotour deep into the marsh. The four of us, along with our guide, set out from the dock shortly after 9 AM. Trumpeter swans were some of the first animals we encountered. There were also Canada geese, and songbirds were everywhere. We also saw a sandhill crane, and several double-crested cormorants made our canoe trip even more special. These unfairly persecuted, native birds are another success story as they were

sandhill crane

almost extirpated from the Great Lakes by the early 1970s largely as a result of DDT and other pesticide use.

As we canoed farther into the marsh, we came across animals including a painted turtle, a northern leopard frog, an eastern gartersnake and a turkey vulture. Two white-tailed deer slowly came to the river and watched us from a distance as we paddled by. Next, two muskrats swam across the river as we quietly sat in

muskrat

the canoe watching them. We stopped and went ashore at a place where we could observe, in the distance, a great blue heron rookery. It was amazing to watch these birds take off from and land in their nests.

Other birds we observed while canoeing deep into the marsh included barn swallows, tree swallows, common mergansers, mallards, marsh wrens, yellow warblers and red-winged blackbirds. We encountered northern watersnakes and two snapping turtles, as well.

Lynn and I also visited Wye Marsh in February, when we walked into the marsh on the boardwalk. It was a sunny day but quite cold as the wind whipped across the marsh. Even though the wind was strong and cold, being in the marsh on a winter's day was an exhilarating experience.

24

There is always plenty for families to do at Wye Marsh. Our family left the marsh with a better understanding of the roles wetlands play and the considerable challenges and threats facing these ecosystems. We certainly felt a greater urgency to protect wetlands and the incredible, precious plants and animals who live there.

● *Gleannan and Liam read about trumpeter swans*

Georgian Bay Islands National Park

Leave it as it is.

The ages have been at work on it and man can only mar it.

—Theodore Roosevelt

AT A GLANCE

- Situated along the east shore of Georgian Bay, from Honey Harbour to Twelve Mile Bay, Georgian Bay Islands National Park is Canada's smallest national park.

- The park is approximately 13 square kilometres in size and is composed of 63 islands that stretch approximately 50 kilometres from Beausoleil Island in the south to Twelve Mile Bay in the north.

- It is only accessible by water, and Beausoleil Island is the only island where you can camp.

- The park has 33 species of reptiles and amphibians—more than any of Canada's other national parks.

- Approximately 800 vascular plant species have been recorded in this park.

25

Directions: Take Highway 400 to Exit 156 for Honey Harbour/Muskoka Road 5. At the stop sign, turn west onto Muskoka Road 5/Honey Harbour Road and proceed for approximately 13 kilometres to Honey Harbour, then watch for the park sign.

website: **www.pc.gc.ca/eng/pn-np/on/georg/ index.aspx**

■ In the quote on the previous page, Theodore Roosevelt was talking about the Grand Canyon, but the subject could just as easily have been Georgian Bay Islands National Park and the rest of the "30,000 Islands"—the planet's largest freshwater archipelago. The ages have been at work creating Georgian Bay and the tens of thousands of islands that are scattered throughout the stunningly beautiful bay.

Much of the park consists of exposed Canadian Shield rock that was formed almost four billion years ago and has been eroded by nature's powerful forces, including the retreating of the glaciers approximately 10,000 years ago. The incredible beauty of this part of the Canadian Shield was made famous by The Group of Seven.

Situated along the east shore of Georgian Bay, from Honey Harbour to Twelve Mile Bay, Georgian Bay Islands National Park is the smallest national park in Canada. The saying "Good things come in small packages" applies to this park. It was created in 1929 when the federal government acquired Beausoleil Island along with 26 smaller islands. At that time, islands in Georgian Bay were being sold and Beausoleil Island was the last remaining large island that was not privately owned.

Over the years the park expanded. Today Georgian Bay Islands National Park is approximately 13 square kilometres in size and comprises 63 islands that stretch 50 kilometres from Beausoleil Island in the south to Twelve Mile Bay in the north. Beausoleil Island is the largest island in the park and is approximately 7 kilometres long by 1.6 kilometres wide.

The island has been home to many indigenous peoples going back thousands of years. Artifacts have been found that date back 7000 years.

25

● *Wetland on Beausoleil Island*

Autumn colours on Beausoleil Island

During the mid-1800s, the Ojibway and Potawatomi people moved to nearby Christian Island from Beausoleil Island. Homesteaders have also lived on Beausoleil Island. Only a few families remained when the island became part of the national park in 1929, and they were assisted in establishing themselves off the island.

A glimpse of the human history on the island is contained in Cemetery of the Oak located near Cedar Spring in the southern portion of the island. The simple grave markers, some dating back to the mid-19th century, mark the graves of young and old residents of the island.

Although Georgian Bay Islands National Park is not large, it contains a diverse ecology. The park has 33 species of reptiles and amphibians—more than any of Canada's other national parks.

Approximately 800 vascular plant species have also been recorded in this park, which is part of the Georgian Bay Littoral Biosphere Reserve. Recognized by the United Nations Educational,

25

Cemetery of the Oak

Scientific and Cultural Organization (UNESCO), the reserve is one of only 13 such reserves in Canada. It is home to more than a hundred at-risk species of animals and plants.

Within the park, biodiversity increases as you go from the outer islands towards the inner islands. The outer islands are exposed to the harsh elements while protecting the middle islands and these, in turn, offer shelter to the inner islands and the mainland, which have high diversity. Because the park lies on the edge of the Canadian Shield, it is home to both northern and southern species of plants and animals.

The northern part of the park is composed of islands with little soil, and the plant life includes lichens, grasses and shrubs, along with some dwarfed trees.

The southern part of Beausoleil Island features thick till layers left behind when the glaciers retreated. These soils support beautiful forests of maple, beech and oak. Besides hardwood and mixed forests, the southern part of the park also contains meadows and wetlands.

Harsh conditions, isolation from the mainland and little soil are some reasons why the outer islands of the park contain considerably less plant life than the park's middle and inner islands. Animal life on these more desolate islands includes such birds as yellow warblers, song sparrows and spotted sandpipers. Herring gulls and common terns nest in colonies on the islands. The northern watersnake is a reptile species

yellow warbler

25

● *An outer island landscape*

● *Forked three-awned grass*

that is also found here. There are virtually no mammals on the outer islands. The colder water surrounding these islands is home to numerous species of fish including lake whitefish and lake trout.

Georgian Bay Islands National Park is home to numerous species of reptiles and amphibians that are listed as either special concern, threatened or endangered. One species that receives considerable attention and protection in the park is the eastern massasauga rattlesnake. This misunderstood and persecuted animal is Ontario's only venomous snake. Habitat protection and educating the public about this typically shy and docile snake are two

rattlesnake

important park initiatives that will help to protect this reptile. The eastern fox-snake is an endangered species found in the park. Humans, habitat loss and development are three threats this snake is exposed to.

One of the bird species being assisted in the park is the osprey. As with the double-crested cormorant, the osprey population around the Great Lakes was devastated by DDT and other toxic contaminants during the 1960s and 1970s. To provide ospreys with more nesting sites near Beausoleil Island, the Georgian Bay Osprey Society has constructed some nest platforms.

Of the plants in the park, one that is considered rare and endangered is the forked three-awned grass. Beausoleil Island and nearby Christian Island are two of only five known areas in Canada where this grass has been found.

Georgian Bay Islands National Park is accessible only by water. If you don't have your own boat, you can go to Beausoleil Island on the park's DayTripper vessel, which departs from Honey Harbour at various times and allows visitors approximately four hours to enjoy the island. The DayTripper goes to Chimney Bay and Cedar Springs, which is the main access point on the island and has wheelchair access.

Although you can explore all the islands by day, Beausoleil Island is the only island in the park where you can camp. It has numerous campgrounds that offer varied camping experiences, from secluded sites to those that are ideal for families as well as wheelchair accessible sites. Rentable rustic cabins have recently been added to Beausoleil Island for those who want a little more comfort during their stay on the island.

Visitors to Beausoleil Island will find many activities to keep themselves busy while they take in the incredible surroundings. Some of the permitted activities include swimming, cycling, hiking, photography, canoeing, kayaking, bird watching and nature appreciation. An impressive trail system has many trails including the Huron Trail that starts at Beausoleil Point in the south and extends north for much of the island. Trails vary in length from just over 250 metres for the Portage Trail to more than 8 kilometres for the Huron Trail.

We have been to Georgian Bay Islands National Park on numerous occasions,

25

● *Gray Island*

in both summer and fall. Lynn and I first went to the park in August and had the opportunity to visit Beausoleil Island as well as some of the other uninhabited islands, including Gray Island, one of the outer islands. Our first destination after leaving Honey Harbour was Honeymoon Bay. Located at the north end of Beausoleil Island, Honeymoon Bay is a scenic spot that features topography typical of central Ontario with lots of rocks and pine trees. A short walk inland took us to two inland lakes—Goblin Lake and Fairy Lake.

Next, we headed to Gray Island, which is part of the Pine Island Group and is located approximately 20 kilometres northwest of Honey Harbour. Gray Island isn't always accessible because it is the park's farthest island from shore—some 6 kilometres or more from the mainland.

Being an outer island and exposed to the elements, Gray Island doesn't have the biodiversity found on the inner islands. We spent close to two hours on the fascinating piece of rock

● *Gray Island*

25

with various shrubs and other plants, but we would have liked to stay much longer. Lynn and I enjoyed all areas of the island, from the barren parts where waves crashed against the rocks to the sheltered coves with their wildflowers and shrubs. We won't forget our visit to this special island.

After visiting Gray Island, we headed to Island 221, located close to the mainland. There was more vegetation than on Gray Island, and some of the rock formations are impressive. After a short visit, we headed back to Beausoleil Island, passing through Little Dog Channel on our way to Cedar Spring. We passed some yachts with their large wakes. Visitors may prefer to canoe

or kayak in the park in late August or September when boat traffic is less busy than it is in the middle of summer. After a brief visit at Cedar Spring we returned to the Parks Canada dock in Honey Harbour.

Our next summer visit to Georgian Bay Islands National Park involved hiking Beausoleil Island. Lynn and I wanted to introduce Liam and Gleannan to this wonderful place. We started in the southern portion of the island and took the Huron Trail north, switching to the Rockview Trail, which took us to Fairy Lake. It was interesting to see the subtle changes as we hiked from south to north on the island. Our hike began in mature deciduous forests of

25

● *Plants grow in sheltered areas of Gray Island*

● *Fairy Lake on Beausoleil Island*

oak and maple in the south, where there was lots of soil, and ended on the rocky, windswept pine landscapes made famous by The Group of Seven. Along the way we encountered some beautiful wetland areas. After hiking, we cooled off in Georgian Bay before returning to Honey Harbour.

Lynn and I wanted to see Beausoleil Island in fall when the trees were beginning to change colour, and we weren't disappointed. On one fine October day we had a chance to hike the Lookout Trail and visit various other parts of the island where some leaves were beginning to turn yellow, orange and red while other trees were already dressed in their fall finest.

Our most recent visit to Beausoleil was again in summer. Our family hiked the trails near Cedar Spring, visited the

Cemetery of the Oak and met an eastern hog-nosed snake, which is a threatened species, before having a swim at a Cedar Spring beach and returning home.

For more than four decades I have been travelling past this water-access park on the way to my parents' cottage on Georgian Bay. Only recently did Lynn and I begin visiting this incredible park. As soon as we end one visit, we are already looking forward to the next time that we will return to Georgian Bay Islands National Park.

eastern hog-nosed snake

Oak Ridges Moraine

In democratic societies people may think that their government
is bound by an ecological version of the Hippocratic oath,
to take no action that knowingly endangers biodiversity.
But that is not enough. The commitment must be much deeper—
to let no species knowingly die, to take all reasonable action
to protect every species and race in perpetuity.

—Edward O. Wilson

AT A GLANCE

- The Oak Ridges Moraine is approximately 170 kilometres long and from 2 to 30 kilometres wide.

- This environmentally sensitive, unique landform is 150 metres deep and consists of a variety of habitats. It performs many functions including acting as a water recharge and discharge area that maintains the health of many watersheds.

- The moraine has approximately 275 kilometres of main trail as well as side trails.

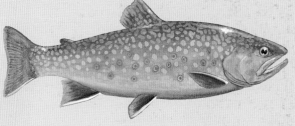

Directions: The Oak Ridges Moraine Trail has numerous access points.

 website: **www.oakridgestrail.org**

OAK RIDGES TRAIL

ORTA

BUILT AND MAINTAINED BY VOLUNTEERS
OBSERVE TRAIL USERS' CODE

· STAY ON THE TRAIL
· KEEP DOGS ON A LEASH
· PROTECT TREES, CROPS AND WILDLIFE
· USE STILES TO CROSS FENCES
· CARRY OUT ALL LITTER
· TAKE NOTHING BUT PHOTOGRAPHS
· LEAVE ONLY YOUR THANKS

OAK RIDGES TRAIL ASSOCIATION
P.O. BOX 28544 AURORA, ONTARIO L4G 0S6

● *Sign at Ballycroy Tract West section of the Oak Ridges Moraine Trail*

Extending from the Trent River system near Rice Lake in the east to the Niagara Escarpment near Caledon in the west, the Oak Ridges Moraine is approximately 170 kilometres long and from 2 to 30 kilometres wide. The geological landform, consisting of hilly terrain, crosses 32 municipalities with more than half of it lying within the Greater Toronto Area.

This environmentally sensitive landform consists of a variety of habitats and performs many functions including acting as a water recharge and discharge area that maintains the health of many watersheds. The Oak Ridges Moraine consists of streams, kettle lakes, ponds, springs, wetlands and aquifers, and it covers approximately 190,000 hectares. Water stored in the sand and gravel aquifers is used for drinking water by municipalities. The aquifers also release water into numerous watercourses that flow north and south into Lake Ontario, Lake Simcoe, Rice Lake and

Lake Scugog as well as Georgian Bay. Water deep within the aquifers originated from glaciers and is thousands of years old.

The Oak Ridges Moraine was created approximately 10,000 to 12,000 years ago when glaciers melted, leaving behind the ridge that is the moraine. When glaciers melt, they leave behind rock fragments and other material that they have been carrying. Where the deposits are thickest, at the glacier's end and sides, are moraines of sand and gravel.

Besides its importance in protecting watersheds, the Oak Ridges Moraine features various habitats that are home to numerous plant and animal species, including many species at risk such as the West Virginia butterfly, the red-shouldered hawk and American ginseng. Brook trout, a good indicator species for water quality, reside in streams on the Oak Ridges Moraine.

Some of the habitats found on the moraine

red-shouldered hawk

include wetlands, forests, meadows, streams, kettle lakes and even some prairie and savannah. Much of the forest that once grew on the moraine has been cut down, but a large forested section still remains. The forest consists largely of maple and beech trees. Many parts of the moraine have been designated as Environmentally Significant Areas (ESAs) and Areas of Natural and Scientific Interest (ANSIs).

Because it is located near Toronto, the biggest threat facing the Oak Ridges Moraine has been development. Subdivisions, roads and other projects

● *Trail near the millpond*

26

that have cleared and paved over sections of the moraine affect how this important landform performs its functions. Changing and damaging the moraine's surface prevents water from entering the hydrologic cycle, reducing water in the aquifers and causing erosion in other areas. Municipalities, golf courses and other large demands for water further affect the moraine.

The ecological value of the Oak Ridges Moraine was recognized in 2001 with the passage of the Oak Ridges Moraine Conservation Act. Unfortunately, much of the moraine is still threatened, including rare prairie grassland, savannah, waterways and many species. The future of the Oak Ridges Moraine will depend largely on a public that recognizes this landform's importance in providing us with a source of water, other species with crucial habitat as well as a green corridor to travel through, and

the environment with a variety of reasonably healthy ecosystems.

A good way to learn about the moraine is to hike it. Experiencing this special piece of southern Ontario up close will provide you with a greater respect for the moraine and a desire to ensure that it is protected in perpetuity. The non-profit, volunteer organization Oak Ridges Trail Association has created approximately 275 kilometres of main trail along with side trails. In the west, the trail starts with a link to the Bruce Trail north of Mono Mills, and it goes through the Northumberland Forest in the east.

The association publishes the *Oak Ridges Trail Guidebook*, which contains maps, access points, information about points of interest and some history of the moraine.

● *Oak Ridges Moraine trail—Ballycroy Tract West*

It was later in October, as some of the deciduous trees were starting to shed their leaves, when Lynn, Liam and I decided to hike sections of the Oak Ridges Moraine Trail. Our first stop was at the north end of the town of Palgrave on Highway 50, just south of Highway 9. We parked in the Palgrave Rotary Park parking lot, near a scenic millpond and a dam, and hiked part of the Palgrave Mill Pond Trail, the site of a flour and gristmill until 1962, and the adjacent Palgrave Forest and Wildlife Area, owned and managed by Toronto and Region Conservation Authority. At this location, the Oak Ridges Moraine Trail goes through cedar, spruce and maple woods next to the West Humber River. We would have liked to hike the section of the Oak Ridges Moraine Trail immediately to the northwest, but it started raining and we decided to save this hike for another day. Although we had driven by this area numerous times, we didn't know that a trail existed here.

The footpath goes by wetlands and along the river. Thanks to its easy access and beautiful scenery, we'll be stopping to hike this section of the Oak Ridges Moraine Trail again when we are in the area.

After hiking this pleasant trail we headed northwest to Adjala/Tosorontio Concession 5 north of Highway 9 and hiked the Ballycroy Tract West section of the Oak Ridges Moraine Trail. Many of the deciduous trees had lost their leaves, which covered the trail, but there were still trees with leaves of various colours, adding to this fall hike. With area parks often packed when autumn colours are at their peak, this section of the Oak Ridges Moraine Trail through a stunning hardwood forest is a more peaceful alternative.

We know just how important the unique, environmentally sensitive Oak Ridges Moraine is. The question is, will we be intelligent enough to protect it?

26

● *Millpond near Palgrave Rotary Park*

Rouge Park

Those who contemplate the beauty of the Earth find reserves of strength that will endure as long as life lasts. There is symbolic as well as actual beauty in the migration of birds, the ebb and flow of tides, the folded bud ready for spring. There is something infinitely healing in the repeated refrains of nature—the assurance that dawn comes after night and spring after the winter.

—Rachel Carson

AT A GLANCE

- Rouge Park is a large natural environment park located in east Toronto as well as York Region and the western part of Pickering.

- At over 40 square kilometres in size, this urban wilderness park is more than 13 times the size of Central Park in New York City.

- The scenic greenbelt provides a corridor for plant and animal populations to live and travel.

- More than 60 species of damselflies and dragonflies have been observed in Rouge Park, including numerous provincially rare species.

- Parts of this large, scenic wilderness park are accessible by public transit.

27

Directions: There are numerous access sites to Rouge Park.

 website: **www.rougepark.com**

Preserving wilderness whenever possible is an important and noble deed that becomes increasingly more urgent as our "progress" includes paving over the environment, threatening species diversity and ecosystems in the process. Because most development occurs in urban areas, protecting pockets of wilderness left in these places is vital.

Rouge Park is a large natural environment park located in east Toronto as well as York Region and the western part of Pickering. At over 40 square kilometres, this urban wilderness park is more than 13 times the size of Central Park in New York City. It protects the watersheds of the Rouge River, Petticoat Creek and Duffins Creek. Rouge Park

● *Little Rouge Creek*

27

extends from Lake Ontario in the south, where there is the Rouge Beach and Marsh, to just south of the Oak Ridges Moraine in the north.

The scenic greenbelt provides a corridor for plant and animal populations, and it links to other greenspace systems, providing further corridors for species to use. Habitats within the park include river valleys, marshes, creeks, meadows and forests. Rouge Park also contains important and rare Carolinian habitat.

The variety of habitats and the sheer size of the park ensure good biodiversity. Close to 800 plant species have been recorded in the section of Rouge Park south of Steeles Avenue, including nationally and regionally rare species.

More than 225 species of birds have also been recorded in the park, which is an important stopover area for migrating birds. Many of the species of birds found in Rouge Park are rare or birds of special concern, as well.

Other animals are also well represented in this near-urban park—more than 60 species of damselflies and dragonflies, 55 species of fish, 27 mammal species and 19 reptile and amphibian species have been recorded in past years, including vulnerable and rare species.

Unfortunately, many species at risk that had been seen in the park have not been observed in recent years.

There are lots of low-impact recreational activities in Rouge Park including numerous hiking trails that vary from 250 metres in length to more than 3 kilometres. Camping is allowed at the Glen Rouge Campground. Picnicking and cycling are also allowed in some areas. Bird watching is another activity that is popular in Rouge Park. To protect the park's flora and fauna, hikers must stay on the signed, marked hiking trails. Cyclists must use areas designated for bikes and are not allowed on the trails.

A nice feature of this large, scenic wilderness park is that parts of it are accessible by public transit, making it convenient for the large, and growing, population of people who live within an hour of Rouge Park. Some areas of the park are also wheelchair accessible. This accessibility makes it possible for families that live in the city to visit a wilderness area.

The government acknowledged the importance of the Rouge Park area when the Province of Ontario created the park in 1994. Since its creation,

Rouge Park has grown considerably, and more exciting things are in store for this wilderness park. A recent addition is the Bob Hunter Memorial Park. Located in the Markham section of the Rouge Park, and named after the environmentalist and author, Bob Hunter Memorial Park will see a new network of trails as well as the creation of a native grass meadow, a wetland and more. Also, as of the writing of this book, Rouge Park is being considered for future national park status. Such an important designation will protect this wilderness corridor from future development.

● *Woodland Trail*

27

It was the end of October when Lynn and I hiked some of Rouge Park. We chose the approximately 2-kilometre Woodland Trail located on Reesor Road just south of Steeles Avenue East. This loop trail goes along Little Rouge Creek for a short distance as well as passing through forests and meadows. The trail was in good condition and easy to hike, making for a nice stroll on a Sunday afternoon. It was well used on this day as evidenced by the nearly full parking lot.

The beginning of the trail is a rock-lined path through a forest. The deciduous trees had shed a significant number of their leaves, which covered the trail. The footpath also went alongside beautiful forests and meadows, which provide important habitat for a variety of species in this largely developed area. Although on the trail there is little evidence that the park is in the middle of a densely populated area, the hydro lines visible at the southeast section of the trail are an indicator of the region's large population and their demand for power.

After leisurely hiking the area for a couple of hours we drove to the site of Bob Hunter Memorial Park, located in eastern Markham in the Cedar Grove Community, because we plan on visiting this part of Rouge Park in the future.

The future of Rouge Park looks bright, especially if it receives national park status. Having such a large, scenic piece of wilderness protected in a densely populated area is rare, and this will ensure that future generations of Canadians in the Greater Toronto Area will have easy access to a stunning piece of the natural world for the foreseeable future.

● *Hydro lines at the southeast section of the Woodland Trail*

27

Tommy Thompson Park

Never doubt that a small group of committed citizens can change the world; indeed, it's the only thing that ever has.

—Margaret Mead

AT A GLANCE

- Tommy Thompson Park is a human-built peninsula, or spit, that extends 5 kilometres south into Lake Ontario.

- More than 300 species of birds have been recorded and ring-billed gulls, black-crowned night-herons, double-crested cormorants and common terns nest in the park in high numbers.

- Within the narrow park, there are various terrestrial and aquatic habitats, including meadows, forests, marshes, sand dunes, beaches, swamps and thickets.

28

Directions: Tommy Thompson Park is located in Toronto at the foot of Leslie Street where it meets Unwin Avenue (south of Lakeshore Boulevard East).

 websites: **www.tommythompsonpark.ca**

www.friendsofthespit.ca

■ I'm not a big fan of urban centres, but I was looking forward to hiking in Tommy Thompson Park (also known as the Leslie Street Spit). Located at the foot of Leslie Street in Toronto, and extending into Lake Ontario, this wilderness area with a unique history came with a good reputation for bird watching.

More than 300 species of birds have been recorded in the park and at least 65 of the species breed here. The park has been designated as a globally significant Important Bird Area and is also considered an Environmentally Significant Area. The park is certainly an important spot for migrating birds to stop, rest and refuel.

Tommy Thompson Park is a human-made peninsula, or spit, that extends 5 kilometres south into Lake Ontario. The life of this special park began in 1959 when the Toronto Harbour Commission (now the Toronto Port Authority) began building the base of the spit. The original role of the peninsula was to protect a new outer harbour, but it later became unnecessary. Material used to create the spit came from construction debris from area development sites as well as dredged material from the Outer Harbour. Tommy Thompson Park is more than 450 hectares and consists of the baselands, a central spine with peninsulas, embayment areas and three cells created between the spine and an endikement to contain contaminated dredging material.

Within the narrow park are various terrestrial and aquatic habitats including meadows, forests, marshes, sand dunes, beaches, swamps and thickets. These habitats constantly change as the young piece of land undergoes natural succession and habitat creation

● *Wetland cells*

by the Toronto and Region Conservation Authority. Wetlands are vital ecosystems, and Toronto and the rest of southern Ontario has lost most of their wetland ecosystems as a result of our activities. The various types of wetlands created on this peninsula don't begin to make up for the wetland destruction we have caused, but it's a step in the right direction.

Although this growing spit of land hasn't been around for a long time, it is home to an impressive number of species. Close to 400 species of plants have been identified in Tommy Thompson Park including rare species such as nodding ladies' tresses. Eastern cottonwood, red-osier dogwood and trembling aspen are common tree species. Some of the plants that you may encounter in the park include Canada thistle, chicory, scouring rush, Canada bluegrass, sandbar willow, lamb's quarters, common reed, common cattail, Richardson's pondweed, white water-lily, Canada goldenrod and New England aster.

Numerous mammals that have found their way to this urban wilderness area include species of mice and bats as well as beavers, foxes, coyotes, muskrats, minks, groundhogs, rabbits, raccoons and squirrels.

Fish of the park include northern pike, largemouth bass, yellow perch and black crappie along with the invasive round goby and common carp.

There is also an impressive list of reptile and amphibian species that visitors many encounter. Turtle species include the midland painted turtle, northern map turtle, Blanding's turtle and the snapping turtle. The milk snake, northern red-bellied snake, DeKay's brown snake and the eastern gartersnake have been observed in the park. There is also

● *A beaver lodge in a wetland*

28

● *A reef raft for nesting common terns*

been initiated to help birds in Tommy Thompson Park. More suitable habitat has been created for shorebirds and other migratory waterbirds, and reef rafts and an island have been created for common terns. A bank was constructed for nesting bank swallows. Bird boxes have been installed for various species including tree swallows.

Numerous species of colonial birds reside within the park. Some, including ring-billed gulls, black-crowned night-herons, double-crested cormorants and common terns, nest in Tommy Thompson Park in high numbers. Other colonial birds found here are great egrets and herring gulls.

black-crowned
night-heron

a population of melanistic (black) eastern gartersnakes. The American toad, northern leopard frog and green frog also reside here.

Numerous species of invertebrates contribute to the park's incredible diversity, including more than 55 species of butterflies as well as numerous species of moths and dragonflies.

While Tommy Thompson Park is home to many plant and animal species, it is best known for the more than 300 species of birds that use this peninsula. Many of the birds in the park are migratory and require the spit for a place to rest and regain their energy before moving on. Others reside here. Colonial waterbirds, songbirds and waterfowl are found in the park in large numbers. Other birds recorded in the park include turkey vultures and various species of hawks, eagles, falcons and owls.

Various projects by the Toronto and Region Conservation Authority have

Because of all the native wildlife, many of which are vulnerable at different times on the spit, the park has a no dogs (or other animal companions) policy. Also, because trucks still bring fill into the park during the week, visitors are only allowed on weekends and many holidays. Permitted activities in the park include hiking, cycling, rollerblading and wildlife viewing. During winter, cross-country skiing and snowshoeing are fun ways to travel in the park.

Although Tommy Thompson Park is an artificially made peninsula, it is an

28

enjoyable and environmentally important place because humans have had a largely hands-off approach since it was created.

Much of the credit for ensuring that this narrow park was left in a primarily "natural" state to be enjoyed by hikers, cyclists and wildlife observers goes to "Friends of the Spit." This effective citizen's advocacy group has been instrumental since 1977 in making sure that the spit has not become a multi-use commercial endeavour and has remained largely an undeveloped piece of wilderness in Toronto. The Toronto and Region Conservation Authority also deserves credit for the way it allows the park to remain a scenic, diverse and natural area.

● *Lighthouse Point*

28

double-crested
cormorant

tree
swallow

Lynn and I visited the park in May when migrating birds were still using the park as a stopover on their way north. We parked our car just outside the park—private vehicles are not permitted when the park is open to the public—and began walking south on Spine Road. Our destination was the lighthouse at Lighthouse Point, located approximately 5 kilometres away. It was a warm day, and walking the paved road surrounded by wilderness next to the downtown Toronto skyline was enjoyable.

There was much to see along the road that extends the length of the peninsula. We encountered snakes, frogs, butterflies and other animals, but what we found incredible was the number of birds we saw.

Double-crested cormorants were almost always overhead carrying material to construct their nests. These large, blue-eyed, mostly black birds alone made our trip to the park worthwhile. Double-crested cormorants are despised in some circles because they nest in large numbers, consume fish and kill some trees that they nest in, but they are native species that play an important role in nature. In fact, they consume large numbers of non-native fish including round gobies, alewives and rainbow smelt. These bids were almost extirpated from the Great Lakes by the early 1970s largely because of DDT and other pesticides; the large numbers of double-crested cormorants in some areas today is to be celebrated as a success story involving a native species. Lynn and I certainly couldn't get enough of these amazing, beautiful birds.

We also saw numerous tree swallows, especially in the areas where there were bird boxes. These attractive birds with their beautiful bluish green feathers were a common and welcome sight during our hike.

There was much to see from the main road, but some short side trails also led

28

to interesting areas. From one lookout area we were able to watch common terns on a reef raft in an embayment area. Turtles and large fish, including common carp, were also visible from this lookout.

Farther up the road we saw stands of large trees that were occupied by large numbers of double-crested cormorants and black-crowned night-herons who were busy building and preparing their nests. What an incredible sight!

We continued on to Lighthouse Point where we admired the beautiful view before turning around and heading back. By then we were tired and hot, but the return hike still held a large

number of opportunities to observe the incredible diversity of plants and animals on this relatively new piece of land. And we kept looking at Toronto's nearby skyline and couldn't get over how close it is to this biologically diverse wilderness area.

After our visit to Tommy Thompson Park, Lynn and I talked about this special park to relatives and friends, and to Gleannan and Liam who could not accompany us on this trip and who are looking forward to visiting this fascinating spit of land soon.

This is one easily accessible big city park I'll be visiting more often.

● *Toronto skyline viewed from the park*

28

Thickson's Woods Nature Reserve

Humanity is cutting down its forests, apparently oblivious to the fact that we may not be able to live without them.

—Isaac Asimov

AT A GLANCE

- Thickson's Woods contains some of the last of the old-growth white pines in the area. These trees were here before European settlers.

- Thickson's Woods Nature Reserve is a sanctuary that provides close to 10 hectares of habitat for numerous species of plants and animals.

Directions: Take Highway 401 to Thickson Road and go south past Wentworth Street. Go past the Waterfront Trail, where there is a sign for Thickson's Wood Nature Reserve on the east side of the road and park at the turnaround.

29

 website: **www.thicksonswoods.com**

Located in Whitby on the north shore of Lake Ontario is Thickson's Woods. Although the woods are only approximately 6.5 hectares in size, they contain some of the last of the old-growth white pines in the area. These trees were growing here before the arrival of European settlers.

Anyone saddened by the loss of local wild areas to development will enjoy, and be inspired by, how Thickson's Woods was saved from chainsaws and bulldozers. This scenic spot was threatened in 1983 when during four days in September more than 60 of the old white pine trees were cut down.

The cutting down of the trees resulted in the creation of Thickson's Woods Heritage Foundation in the spring of 1984, when a small group of citizens came up with a down payment to purchase the property. During the next five years, the foundation raised the remaining money needed to pay off the mortgage by having yard sales and other fund-raising activities as well as receiving donations from supporters who wanted to help protect this important wild area. Donations came from people as far away as England and Japan. The property known as Thickson's Woods not only contains the scenic forest, but also a portion of the Corbett Creek Marsh.

More recently, Thickson's Woods Heritage Foundation purchased a property immediately north of Thickson's Woods. The approximately 3.5-hectare former pasture was also in danger of being developed, so the foundation set to work, and the property is now being allowed to return to a more natural state on its own. The meadow links the valley of Corbett Creek with Thickson's Woods. Together the woods and the meadow are known as Thickson's Woods Nature Reserve, and this sanctuary provides close to 10 hectares of habitat for many species of plants and animals. Besides the impressive white

● *The meadow at Thickson's Woods Nature Reserve*

29

pines, other species of plants found in the reserve include common milkweed, common elderberry, common trillium, red-osier dogwood, butternut, and eastern hemlock. Common loons, red-throated loons, eastern phoebes, great horned owls, great blue herons, wood ducks, belted kingfishers, Carolina wrens, cedar waxwings and pine warblers are only some of the bird species recorded in the reserve. The area is also an important stopover for migrating birds.

Lynn and I visited Thickson's Woods Nature Reserve near the end of September. It was a beautiful morning as we strolled down the Waterfront Trail, which divides Thickson's Woods and the meadow properties. We checked out the meadow first. The grass trail wound through the attractive field that contains shrubs, wildflowers and young trees.

After leisurely hiking the meadow, we headed across the Waterfront Trail and entered Thickson's Woods. A sign informs visitors that the white pines located here "...were once reserved for masts of sailing ships of the British Royal Navy." The forest was beautiful, and we enjoyed hiking the trails through the woods. The towering white pines really are impressive. Besides the woods and meadow, we hiked along the Waterfront Trail and enjoyed the view over Corbett Creek Marsh from a bridge, where we watched a great blue heron and some other birds.

In a time when development and paving over the environment usually wins out over protecting vital ecosystems, it is both comforting and inspiring to learn that some islands of remaining wilderness can be saved. Thanks to the efforts of concerned citizens, Thickson's Woods Nature Reserve is one such place.

● *Waterfront Trail*

29

Presqu'ile Provincial Park

Whatever befalls the earth befalls the sons of the earth.
Man did not weave the web of life; he is merely a strand in it.
Whatever he does to the web, he does to himself.

—Chief Seattle

AT A GLANCE

- Presqu'ile Provincial Park is a 937-hectare park that is on a peninsula south of Brighton that also includes Gull Island and High Bluff Island.

- Monarch Butterflies visit Presqu'ile in large numbers, arriving in early June. Autumn in the park sees the fall migration of these fascinating animals. Close to 70 species of butterflies have been recorded in Presqu'ile Provincial Park.

- More than 330 species of birds, including numerous species at risk, have been recorded in the park.

- The variety of habitats within the park, which includes marshes, dunes, sand and cobble beaches, fields and forests, leads to an incredible diversity of species.

Directions: From Brighton take Main Street (Regional Road 2) to Ontario Street. Turn south on Ontario Street, which becomes Presqu'ile Parkway, and proceed to the park.

website: **www.ontarioparks.com/english/pres.html**

www.friendsofpresquile.on.ca

30

Located on the north shore of Lake Ontario between Toronto and Kingston is Presqu'ile Provincial Park. The 937-hectare park is on a peninsula south of Brighton that also includes Gull Island and High Bluff Island.

Presqu'ile is French for "almost an island," and this scenic peninsula was once a limestone island similar to Gull Island and High Bluff Island. It took hundreds of years, but sand-pits from the mainland and the outer island grew towards each other forming a tombolo—a barrier beach that joins the mainland and a former island together. The Presqu'ile tombolo is the best example of a tombolo on the Great Lakes and includes numerous habitats including a sand beach, dunes, a sea-sonally wet meadow and points going into Presqu'ile Bay Marsh known as "The Fingers."

Presqu'ile Park was established in 1922 and was managed by Presqu'ile Park Commission. In 1955, the Presqu'ile Provincial Commission was dissolved and the park, now known as Presqu'ile Provincial Park, was regulated by an Order of Council under the Provincial Parks Act. Today the park is managed by Ontario Parks, which is part of the Ontario Ministry of Natural Resources.

Presqu'ile Provincial Park is a natural environment park, and its important features have been recognized with such designations as a globally significant Important Bird Area (IBA), a Wetland of International Importance, an Area of Natural and Scientific Interest (ANSI) and as a Monarch Butterfly Reserve. The Monarch Butterfly is a species of special concern in Canada.

The variety of habitats within the park, which includes marshes, dunes, sand and cobble beaches, fields and forests, leads to an incredible diversity of species. Presqu'ile Provincial Park is probably best known for the birds who use

● *Chestnut-sided warbler*

the park—either as a home or as a stop-over area while migrating. More than 330 species of birds, including numerous species at risk, have been recorded in the park, with approximately 120 species known to breed here.

There are many reasons for the numerous bird species and the large numbers of birds who visit Presqu'ile, including the park's diversity of habitats, its location and its shape. Situated on one of the Great Lakes, which pose a barrier to birds migrating over them, Presqu'ile's peninsula that sticks out into the lake offers birds the first place to rest. The diversity of habitats ensures that most birds will find food and shelter in the park.

Monarch Butterflies also visit Presqu'ile in large numbers, arriving in early June, where they lay their eggs on milkweed plants. Autumn in the park sees the fall migration of these animals. Close to 70 species of butterflies have been recorded in Presqu'ile.

Presqu'ile Provincial Park is also home to a population of white-tailed deer along with numerous species of reptiles and amphibians.

Besides watching Presqu'ile's impressive animal life, you can enjoy many other recreational activities in the park, including camping; the campground areas offer hundreds of sites. The long beach offers good swimming opportunities, and photography and picnicking are also popular activities.

For those who enjoy hiking, there are seven trails within the park, the shortest of which are the Lighthouse Foot Path and the Cemetery Trail at 300 metres. The Marsh Boardwalk is a 1.2-kilometre loop trail through a marsh that features two observation towers. The Owen Point Trail is a 1.6-kilometre loop along a sandy path that goes near birding areas. The Pioneer Trail (3.8-kilometre loop) and the Newcastle Trail (3-kilometre loop) go through forest, field and plantations of spruce, pine and tamarack.

Jobes' Woods Trail is a beautiful one-kilometre loop that goes through such habitats as old growth forest, swamp forests and old fields. In 1835, this land was settled by Thomas and Ezekiel Jobes.

● *A boardwalk in Jobes' Woods*

white-tailed deer

30

● *Presqu'ile Lighthouse*

● *Shore of Lake Ontario within the park*

A bicycle trail also exists within the park, and in winter, cross-country skiing and snowshoeing are allowed.

Complementing Presqu'ile's recreational opportunities is its history, which includes shipwrecks, pirates, rumrunners and more. The park also has one of the province's oldest lighthouses. Built in 1840, the Presqu'ile Lighthouse was constructed of limestone. In 1894, the lighthouse was wrapped in timber and sided with cedar shingles to protect the stone and mortar structure from the elements.

Helping with the park's educational and fund raising initiatives is the volunteer organization The Friends of Presqu'ile Park.

It was with mixed feelings that I thought of visiting Presqu'ile Provincial Park. I'd heard that the park was a particularly scenic one with an impressive diversity of plants and animals. I also knew that double-crested cormorants were "managed" in past years by killing large numbers of these birds, many of whom suffered terribly. White-tailed deer have also been killed in this park to reduce their numbers.

I disagree with the idea that native species need to be managed. Animals live in harmony with their environment. The return of the double-crested cormorant is a success story to be celebrated. These birds were almost extirpated from the Great Lakes Basin because of pesticides, other toxic chemicals and human persecution. Although their

30

numbers have rebounded significantly in recent decades, their populations will only grow until they reach the carrying capacity of their environment, which is determined by limiting factors such as space and food. Then their numbers will level off or decrease, something that is already happening to Great Lakes cormorant populations. The double-crested cormorant is an indicator species. A healthy population of these birds indicates that the environment is also healthy.

Lynn and I went to Presqu'ile in late September, arriving in the park early in the afternoon. It was a nice, warm day. The park contains a variety of habitats, but its wetlands caught our interest first, and we headed for the Marsh Boardwalk Trail, which takes you through the marsh and ends with a walk through a beautiful cedar forest. Viewing towers and interpretive signs complement the trail that consists largely of a boardwalk, which has been rebuilt by The Friends of Presqu'ile Park, through the marsh. On this trail we saw northern leopard frogs, mute swans, ducks and dragonflies including some band-winged meadowhawks.

Our next stop was the Owen Point Trail, a 1.6-kilometre loop that offers good bird watching opportunities. The trail is a sandy path with lookouts to view migrating shorebirds along the beach. To avoid disturbing migrating birds you cannot access the beach, and animal companions are not permitted on this trail. We were hoping to see a variety of shorebirds, but there were actually very few—possibly as a result of the waterfowl hunt that occurred the previous day. This trail did offer good viewing opportunities for other animals—frogs, snakes and songbirds were always nearby. The area also had monarch butterflies and other butterflies enjoying the wildflowers in bloom.

Next, we drove along Lighthouse Lane, where we visited a picnic area on our way to Presqu'ile Point to see the lighthouse.

Although we could have spent days enjoying the trails, habitats and activities of this park, our day trip was coming to an end. Before leaving the park we wanted to hike one more trail—the Jobes' Woods Trail. The short trail contains some magnificent maple trees and other mature deciduous trees and features a nice footpath with sections of boardwalk. Our stroll through the woods was a nice way to finish our short stay in Presqu'ile Provincial Park.

● *Northern Leopard Frog*

30

Some Final Thoughts

In wildness is the preservation of the world.

–Henry David Thoreau

■ Our family thoroughly enjoyed visiting the wilderness areas featured in this book. I was surprised at the number of natural areas that exist within a short drive of our home. The more I looked into places to visit, the more places I discovered.

While I was pleasantly surprised at the number of parks, conservation areas and other places to enjoy nature that exist in south-central Ontario, I was also disturbed at how our "progress" has included paving over and destroying the natural environment that existed in this part of the province not so long ago. The beautiful parks and trails that we visited are surrounded by urban areas, literally making these wilderness areas islands within a sea of development. With the population rapidly increasing in this part of the province, we need more and larger nature areas, like Rouge Park, to protect the environment, including plants and animals, and to ensure that we have natural places to go seek solace and peace.

New parks and trails need to be created and existing parks should be expanded whenever possible. If larger boundaries cannot be realized, then buffer areas should be created by purchasing properties on the edges of the parks, conservation areas and trails when the land becomes available.

There are some bright spots, however, as the Bruce Trail and the Oak Ridges Moraine Trail act as green corridors that link natural areas to one another. These corridors provide us with wonderful recreational opportunities. More importantly, they provide plants and animals with long, unfragmented territory where they can live, breed and travel.

Smaller trails that extend for considerable distances linking nature areas also exist and include the Elora Cataract Trailway, the Georgian Trail and the Tom Thomson Trail. These trails not only provide some natural areas that link to other natural areas, but they also provide people with places to travel in an eco-friendly manner.

Hope also exists with concerned citizens who are dedicated to protecting the environment and making it available for the public to enjoy, such as those who organized the purchase of Thickson's Woods and who maintain the Trout Hollow Trail.

I have been impressed with many of the parks and conservation areas that keep their properties in a largely natural state, such as with Tommy Thomson Park and Georgian Bay Islands National Park, or are even returning some parks to a more natural environment, such as with Terra Cotta Conservation Area.

I am also optimistic that we are, slowly, learning about the importance of habitats such as wetlands and the need to protect these areas. Unfortunately, money usually wins out over common sense and protecting the environment. As I write this, vital ecosystems in south-central and central Ontario are at risk from proposed quarries and other developments—including a plan to allow mining that would destroy old-growth forest near Temagami.

We have already decimated much of the wilderness of southern and central Ontario. Any pockets of relatively untouched wilderness that have not been despoiled must be protected, and red pine trees that have been around for several hundred years certainly fall into this category.

Destroying such sacred areas for economic reasons should not be allowed to happen, and all levels of government need to do much more to ensure that future generations of all species, including ours, have a pristine, natural environment to enjoy. When governments fail to act responsibly by protecting such wilderness areas, it is up to us to ensure that they do the right thing.

I am also disappointed—angry is more like it—that hunting is allowed in some of the areas featured in this book. I considered these pieces of wilderness to be havens or sanctuaries for the animals who live in, and migrate through, them. Welcoming animals for most of the year and then shooting them during specified periods is wrong.

Although the vast majority of southern Ontario's wilderness no longer exists, there are still scattered remnants of this once-magnificent landscape. Other areas are being allowed to return to a more natural state. Many of these tracts of forests, wetlands, meadows and other habitats can be experienced by hiking or canoeing and through other eco-friendly activities.

Visit these special wilderness areas and take your family. You can't help but enjoy and respect these incredible places, and these feelings will result in a desire to protect them. The more people use these areas and act to protect them, the more we can ensure that the region's rich biodiversity remains and that the incredible wilderness that defines Ontario is protected forever.

About the Author

GLENN PERRETT has a degree in Environmental Studies from the University of Waterloo. He has written nearly 200 articles on animals and the environment that have appeared in magazines such as *Homes and Cottages*, *Pets Magazine* and *Muskoka Magazine*, as well as in many newspapers. He and his family—wife Lynn and children Gleannan and Liam—hike, canoe, cross-country ski and photograph wilderness areas throughout the year.